IN QUIETNESS & CONFIDENCE

THE MAKING OF A MAN OF GOD

David Roper

DISCOVERY HOUSE
PUBLISHERS®

Feeding the Soul with the Word of God

In Quietness and Confidence
© 1999 by David Roper
All rights reserved.

Discovery House Publishers is affiliated with RBC Ministries, Grand Rapids, Michigan.

Requests for permission to quote from this book should be directed to: Permissions Department, Discovery House Publishers, P.O. Box 3566, Grand Rapids, MI 49501, or contact us by e-mail at permissionsdept@dhp.org

All Scripture quotations, unless otherwise indicated, are taken from the Holy Bible, New International Version®, NIV®. Copyright ©1973, 1978, 1984 by Biblica, Inc.™ Used by permission of Zondervan. All rights reserved worldwide. www.zondervan.com

ISBN 978-1-57293-749-9

Printed in the United States of America
Third printing in 2013

FOR CAROLYN

Steel-true and blade-straight
The great artificer
made my mate. . . .

Teacher, tender, comrade, wife,
A fellow-farer true through life,
Heart-whole and soul-free
The august father
Gave to me.

—Robert Louis Stevenson

CONTENTS

"In quietness and confidence is your strength."

—Isaiah 30:15

THE VIEW FROM THE SOUTH FORK . . .
AND OTHER THINKING SPOTS

I have found it to be a real truth that
the very sitting by the river's edge is not
only the quietest and fittest place for
contemplation, but will invite an angler to
do it.

—Izaak Walton

THERE'S A TROUT STREAM ABOUT AN HOUR AWAY FROM BOISE, Idaho, known locally as "The South Fork." No other designation is needed; every fly fisherman in the valley knows it by that name.

It's been known to offer up some fair-sized trout now and then, but it's a capricious river. I've fished it with might and main on days when all the conditions were exactly, or seemed exactly, right and have caught exactly nothing.

But no matter. When the fishing falls off I find a place to sit and enjoy the solitude. It's a quiet zone in the midst of my much-too-busy world, a place to lift my eyes from my crowded existence to the "eternal hills," to live for a brief time a less-annoyed life. It's one of my "thinking spots" as Winnie the Pooh would say.

Izaak Walton, author of *The Compleat Angler* (1653), said that rivers are made for wise men to contemplate and only fools pass by them without consideration. While I'm no sage, I do agree that rivers invite periods of quiet thought. I'd be a fool not to take advantage of them. The South Fork is just such a place. And what follows in these pages are a few of the ideas that have come to me there and in other tranquil places I know.

It is said that when French mathematician and theologian Blaise Pascal died, his family found his study and pockets littered with small scraps of paper on which he had jotted down his ideas. They were collected into what later became known as *Pensées* (Thoughts). With apologies to Pascal, these are some of my *pensées*—random thoughts I've written on scraps of paper at various times and have finally gotten around to collecting and reworking into the ideas you'll find in this book.

All have to do with spiritual formation, that process by which Christ is formed in us—for our sake, for God's sake, and for the sake of others. Some are long; others are short; all are incomplete. I agree with children's writer Katherine Peterson: "We cannot go back and revise our lives, but being allowed to go back and revise what we have written comes closest." Someday I'm sure I'll want to gather up these thoughts and revise them, because spiritual understanding, like every other living thing, is always growing.

The format for this book is simple: there is one chapter for each day of the month, and each chapter contains a Scripture selection and a brief essay based on that text. It is my hope that you'll read the Scripture text and essay each morning, ponder both through the day, and pray the truth, as it comes to you, into your soul.

It is my prayer that these writings will speak to your heart and not just to your head. As Bunyan wrote in his preface to *The Pilgrim's Progress*, "Lay my book, thy head, and heart together."

David Roper
Boise, Idaho

CHAPTER 1 | THE QUIET MAN

I have discovered that all human evil comes from this, man's being unable to sit still in a room.

—BLAISE PASCAL

READ Psalm 131

A FISHING BUDDY OF MINE RECENTLY PASSED ON TO ME A SLIM volume entitled *Fishin' Jimmy*. It was written in 1889 by New Englander Anne Trumbull Slosson. It's about a man who lived in Franconia, that little valley in New Hampshire made famous by Nathaniel Hawthorne's *The Great Stone Face*.

Fishin' Jimmy was an angler who fly-fished the streams and ponds of that region for over half a century. I was immediately intrigued by the story, because some years ago Carolyn and I camped in Franconia Notch, and I fished those very streams.

Fishin' Jimmy was a genial, kindly, accessible man, a lover of men and women, boys and girls, a friend of publicans and sinners. He was a simple man with a deep faith who walked with God in the quietness of his own soul.

One thing troubled Jimmy, however. He wanted to become a "fisher of men." That was what the Great Teacher had promised those first fishermen who left their boats to follow him.

"I allers try to think that 't was me in that boat when he come along," Jimmy muses. "I'd make b'l'eve that it was out on Streeter's Pond, an' I was settin' in the boat, fixin' my lan'in' net, when I see him on the shore. I think mebbe I'm that James—for that's my given name, ye know, though they allers call me Jimmy—an' then I hear him callin' me, 'James, James.' I can hear him jest plain sometimes, when the wind's blowin' in the trees, an' I jest ache to up an' foller him. But says he, 'I'll make ye a fisher o'men,' an' he ain't done it. I'm waitin'; mebbe he'll larn me some day."

What Fishin' Jimmy did not know is that the Great Teacher had already "larned" him. Jimmy had walked a long time with Jesus and God's gracious ways had rubbed off on him. Fishin' Jimmy had become a center of peace, a man who touched lives profoundly wherever he went, who left behind the unforgettable fragrance of Christ.

David speaks of those like Jimmy who "live quietly" and yet deeply (Psalm 35:20). In every age God has his men who have retired from life's noise and confusion, have withdrawn from its ambitions and jealousies, and have entered into the secret of a life that is hidden in God.

This doesn't mean that these men necessarily escape from life's dangers and dilemmas, but it does mean they have the ability to live with tranquility in the midst of them. Though much trouble may remain, confusion, apprehension, instability, and despair have begun to dwindle away. These are the "quiet men" who show poise under pressure, who are unshaken by life's alarms and who radiate wisdom and peace wherever they go.

> Content to be but little known,
> Content to wander on alone;
> Here—hidden inwardly in Thee;
> Then—light in Thine own light to be.

—Jesse Penn Lewis

Ordinary men, unfamiliar with the hidden depths of God, necessarily live busy, fussy, ambitious, care-ridden lives. They're always fretful, always restless, always looking for that illusive "something more."

But those who have learned to turn their energies toward God can be calm in the hustle and bustle of the marketplace as well as the tedium and weariness of the commonplace, quiet in the midst of life's homeliest duties and excessive demands.

F. B. Meyer says that most of us are like folks living in a one-room house located too close to the street. There's no way to get away from the noise and commotion outside. But we can build a soundproof room within and make it our dwelling place—a secret chamber to ponder God's word and talk things over with him.

"We fill our little space," Meyer says, "we get our daily bread and are content; we enjoy natural and simple pleasures; we do not strive, nor cry, nor cause our voice to be heard in the street; we pass through the world, with noise-less tread, dropping a blessing on all we meet."

It's in that quiet place that we learn peace and bring that peace out to others. George MacDonald, that wise, old Scot, put it this way: "There is a chamber—a chamber in God himself which none can enter but the one, the individual, the particular man. Out of which chamber that man has to bring revelation and strength for his brethren. This is that for which he was made—to reveal the secret things of the Father."

We're distracted because we've lost that orientation, but we can learn again to be quiet. We can take our anxious worry and nervous energy to Jesus. When people disappoint us we can confide in him. When storms sweep over us we can hide in him. When people jostle one another and jockey for position, when they compete for fame and fortune and their passions begin to stir us we can run to that little chamber, shut the door and quiet our hearts again. We can be calm and strong—

> Firm in the right; mild to the wrong;
> Our heart, in every raging throng,
> A chamber shut for prayer and song.
>
> —George MacDonald

CHAPTER 2 | NOT BOTHERING

Never underestimate the value of Doing
Nothing, of just going along, listening
to all the things you can't hear, and not
bothering.

—Winnie the Pooh

READ Jeremiah 17:19–27

"NOT BOTHERING"—I LIKE POOH'S ADVICE. WOULD THAT I, LIKE THAT
wise old bear, could lead a less bothered life.

Jeremiah speaks to that tendency to bother oneself with life's burdens: "Be
careful not to carry a load on the Sabbath," he said. It's an odd text to fix on, but
it sets my mind right. Let me explain.

Jeremiah took his stand in the city gates of Jerusalem, where he could be
heard by all who walked by, and proclaimed this message: "This is what the LORD
says: 'Be careful not to carry a load on the Sabbath day or bring it through the

gates of Jerusalem. Do not bring a load out of your houses or do any work on the Sabbath'" (Jeremiah 17:21–22).

It's odd that Jeremiah would stress Sabbath observance when so much was wrong with the city, but it was essential to do so because the Sabbath is at the heart of what ails us—our tendency to work ourselves to death when God wants to give us rest.

Rest is the oldest institution in the world. It was established in the beginning when God set out to make the world. He worked six days, we're told, and then took a day off. Then God wrote that day large in Israel's law book and on her calendar. He called the day *Sabbath*, a word that means "to cease from one's labors, to rest."

Augustine noted that the phrase "there was evening, and there was morning," which occurs on each of the first six days of creation, is conspicuously absent on the seventh day. The seventh day had a beginning, but it had no end. God's rest goes on forever.

This restful seventh day was a symbolic rule for Israel, but for us now it's a daily reality—that "spiritual rest, in which believers lay aside their own works to allow God to work for them," as John Calvin said. The Sabbath was once a day to rest; now it's an everyday thing (Colossians 2:16–17; Hebrews 4:1–11).

The Sabbath is not a day, it's a disposition—a mindset of resting every day, all day for all we have to accomplish, believing that God is at the heart of all our activity. It's an unencumbered, unhurried, relaxed lifestyle that grows out of a deep awareness that God is on the job twenty-four hours a day whether we are or not.

Solomon wrote, "In vain you rise early and stay up late, toiling for food to eat—for [God] grants sleep to those he loves" (Psalm 127:2).

There's something wonderfully significant about this psalm, something easily missed unless we understand that the Sabbath for Israel began, not on Saturday morning, but on Friday evening at bedtime.

The Hebrew evening and morning sequence says something significant to us: God puts his children to sleep so he can get his work done. "Sleep is God's contrivance for giving us the help he cannot get into us when we are awake," said George MacDonald.

In the evening, fatigue overtakes us and we have to stop working. We lay ourselves down to sleep and drift off into blessed oblivion for the next six to eight hours, a state in which we are totally nonproductive. But nothing essential stops. Though we may leave many things undone, many projects unfinished, God is still at work. "He grants sleep to those he loves." The next morning, his eyes sweep over us and he awakens us to enjoy the benefits of all that he has done.

Most of us, however, hit the floor running. We wolf down a Power Bar and dash out the door with a travel mug of coffee clutched in our hand. We have to be up and doing, getting things started and getting a world of things done. That's because we don't yet understand that God has been working for us all along. We have awakened into a world in which everything was started centuries ago. God has been preparing the good works in which we find ourselves walking each day (Ephesians 2:10).

F. B. Meyer says, "We must remember to maintain within our hearts the spirit of Sabbath calm and peace, not fussy, not anxious, nor fretful nor impetuous; refraining our feet from our own paths, our hand from our own devices, refusing to make our own joy and do our own works. It is only when we are fully resolved to act thus, allowing God to originate his own plans and to work in us for their accomplishment that we enter into rest."

And what keeps us from entering into God's rest? Unbelief. Underlying all our worry and compulsive self-effort is the thought that God cannot or will not come through. That's why the people of Israel wouldn't lay their burdens down in Jeremiah's day and that's why we can't let up. That's why we have to keep hustling and hoping to do more. That's why we get so weary and worn out. That's why we get so worried. And that's why we need to find rest.

Can we do it? You bet your life we can. We can keep the Sabbath inwardly and carry no burdens through the gates of our minds. The necessary is always possible. God never commands without giving us the means to comply.

Here's what we must do: we must greet anxiety at the door with one short, strong answer—"God." We must say to ourselves, as Abraham said to Isaac in his moment of greatest worry, "God will provide" (Genesis 22:8). And then we must leave the matter with him. That's how we enter into his rest.

Paul says the same thing: "Do not be anxious about anything, but in everything, by prayer and petition, with thanksgiving, present your requests to God. And the peace of God, which transcends all understanding, will guard your hearts and your minds in Christ Jesus (Philippians 4:6–7).

Our wills can direct our thoughts to any object they choose. We can either obsess over our fear, or look away from it and direct our thoughts toward God and his perfect solutions. It's good to think objectively about the issues that distress us, but to fret over them is to deny God's love for us and his ability to save.

Some years ago I was walking a stream bed with my brother-in-law, Ed Wichern, accompanied by his son David, who was then about three years old. David was collecting "piglets," as he called them, round stream rocks that did indeed look like Winnie the Pooh's porcine friend.

The accumulation of rocks soon got to be too much for David who struggled along unable to keep up. "Let me carry your piglets, David," Ed said. "No," David replied firmly, "You carry me and I'll carry my piglets."

I couldn't help but think then, and many times since then, how David's childish self-reliance rebukes my own grown-up reluctance to let God take my burdens. "You carry me," I insist, "but all the cares of life are my own." Much better, Peter insists, to cast all our anxiety on him because he cares about us (1 Peter 5:7).

> Rest; rest in Him—
> Your work is through.
> Lean back on his great power;
> He'll work for you.

—John Fischer

CHAPTER 3 | THE OLD TREE

And there is healing in old trees.

—Lord Byron

READ Exodus 15:22–25

MOSES AND ISRAEL HAD SEEN GOD TRIUMPH OVER THE HORSE and its rider and bury the Egyptian army in the sea. They paused for a moment to sing the "Song of Redemption" (Exodus 15:1–18), then marched three days through the vast wasteland of Shur to an old oasis where they expected to find water.

There was water there, but it was bad water, and it left a bitter taste. God's people began to mutter among themselves and murmur against Moses. "What are you going to do now?" they grumbled, "What are we going to drink?" Moses didn't have a clue.

Then the Lord pointed out a tree to Moses—a rugged piece of wood that grew beside the oasis—and told Moses to throw it into the water, which he did, "and the water became sweet" (15:25).

Joy and sorrow are often juxtaposed. How quickly our enjoyment can turn into bitterness. One moment we're singing the Song of Redemption, the next moment we're crying the blues, complaining about our circumstances, muttering over our lot, and allowing the bitterness of the moment to seep into our souls.

The power of these foul moods is that they make the old self seem right in its insistence that we were made for ease and affluence and that present circumstances are depriving us of the good life. "It isn't fair!" we complain, then sulk and pout. We grow more embittered and rancorous with every memory; we lapse into lethargy and depression.

There is, however, a tree which, when cast into our bitter waters, can make them sweet. It is

> The cross on which the Savior died,
>   and conquer'd for his saints,
> This is the tree by faith applied,
>   that sweetens all complaints.

—Alfred Nevin

The cross is that symbol of acceptance, our utter submission to the will of God. The cross means for us what it meant for Christ—to will one thing. As Jesus said when he willingly stretched himself out on his tree, "My Father, if it is possible, may this cup be taken from me. Yet not as I will, but as you will" (Matthew 26:39). This must be our attitude as well. This is what Paul calls "being conformed to his death" (Philippians 3:10).

F. B. Meyer has written, "It is in proportion as we see God's will in the various events of life and surrender ourselves either to bear it or do it, that we shall find earth's bitter circumstances becoming sweet and its hard things easy."

It may be that our bitterness comes from a nagging illness, a difficult marriage, a carping critic that will not go away. It may come from regret and disappointment over what could have been, what would have been, if only someone had been less self-absorbed.

We can sweeten that bitterness if we choose to see each circumstance as God's choice for us and willingly accept it—saying "yes" to him and to his will. He has chosen this difficult place for us; he has permitted this intrusion; it is his will that we are here. "Disappointment is his appointment," someone has said. We too must see it that way.

The painful event may seem cruel and capricious, but it is not; it has been screened through infinite wisdom and love long before it ever got to us. It is not the ill-use of an adversary, but the gracious will of a loving Father and Friend.

Since he is good, God will not leave us in the lurch, nor will he ever forsake us. He will keep us in his love. He will teach us the lessons he intends us to learn. He will work in us the changes he wants us to make. He will give us the grace we need to be brave in the midst of our calamities and behave as his children should. And then in his good time—in this life or in the next—he will deliver us from evil.

And so, as F. B. Meyer says, we are here in this place, whatever it may be, "by [God's] appointment, in his keeping, under his tutelage, for his time." In this we must rest.

> He said, "I will accept the breaking sorrow
> Which God tomorrow
> Will to his son explain."
> Then did the turmoil deep within him cease.
> Not vain the word: vain, vain;
> For in *acceptance* lieth peace.

—Amy Carmichael

CHAPTER 4 | BROKEN CISTERNS

Attempt, how vain—
    with things of earthly sort, with aught
but God,
    to satisfy and fill the immortal soul!

—Robert Pollock

READ Jeremiah 2:1–19

OUR OLD DOG SITS BESIDE ME AS I WRITE, STARING OFF INTO space—a distant, unfocused look in her eyes. A penny for her thoughts.

One thing I'm sure she's not thinking about is the meaning of life. "The Far Side" notwithstanding, dogs don't contemplate what life means; only what it provides. People do, however, and therein lies the rub.

It's not that we want to think about life; it's that we *have* to. Something (or Someone) keeps prompting hard questions about who we are and where we're going—questions that lead us into deeper questions, confusions, and cul-de-sacs.

What's it all about, Alfie? Why am I here? What is my duty? Why work all my life and endure a never-ending round of frustrations when "all my harvest fields," as Francis Thompson said, "are bedunged with rotten death"? Why go on when, no matter what I do, I'm going to end up under the ground?

"You know what's funny?" Dilbert's colleague Ratbert asks. "I'll tell you. You're working hard. I'm doing nothing. In a hundred years we'll both be dead."

"You may not need to wait that long," Dilbert snarls over his shoulder as Ratbert leaves to spread joy in some other place.

Psychoanalyst Erich Fromm makes the point that given the frustrations of our existence, the real question is not why some people lose their minds, but why more people don't. He writes, "Considering man's position in the world, his separateness, aloneness, powerlessness, and his awareness of this, one would expect this burden to be more than he can bear, so that he would literally go to pieces under the strain."

Some folks do go to pieces, of course; they crack up under the strain. Most of us, however, as Fromm goes on to say, "avoid this outcome by compensatory mechanisms like the overriding routine of life, conformity with the herd, the search for power, prestige, and money, dependence on idols. . . . All these compensatory mechanisms can maintain sanity, provided they work—up to a point."

What Fromm is saying is that our thoughts about life and death are so powerful and pervasive that we have to find some way to protect ourselves from them. That's what's behind our drive for money, power, and success. That's why our efforts—whether we're pursuing a Ph.D. in computer science or a black belt in karate—always have a compulsive feel to them. We become single-minded and obsessive in our pursuits so that we can forget about ourselves—so that our anxiety will become less oppressive.

Fromm calls these works "compensatory mechanisms." God calls them "cisterns."

> My people have committed two sins: They have forsaken me, the spring of living water, and have dug their own cisterns, broken cisterns that cannot hold water (Jeremiah 2:13).

Cisterns are mere holes in the ground, reservoirs for storing rainwater. In ancient times they were usually pear-shaped reservoirs with a small opening at the top. Most were small, but some were very large and took a long time and a lot of work to dig. (One excavated in Jerusalem had a capacity of over two million gallons!)

Picture yourself swinging a pick, digging from dawn to dusk, excavating the hard, unyielding ground. While others are playing golf, swimming, fishing, vacationing, gathering with family and friends, you stay on the job, working through the biting cold of winter and through the blazing heat of summer when the sun turns your cistern into a kiln.

After years of strenuous, demanding effort you finally achieve your purpose: you complete the hole on which you've invested your best years. Then you step back and wait for your cistern to fill—and it leaks. There's a crack or flaw in the tank; perhaps the stone is too porous or the lining is faulty and you discover what every one of your neighbors has found, or will find, that cisterns, no matter how well constructed, always leak.

"I'll dig another cistern," you say. "I'll take my project back to the drawing board and draft a new, improved version. I'll work harder, work longer, work somewhere else, make it work this time."

But sooner or later reality settles in. It's just a matter of time. Our projects work "only to a point" Fromm said. In the end we run out of money, energy, time, or some other resource, and every effort becomes meaningless. We "come to the cisterns and find no water; (we) return with our vessels empty" (Jeremiah 14:3). We find ourselves in that state of bitter despair Danish philosopher Søren Kierkegaard described as "the sickness unto death."

You may remember Robert Ringer and his greed-inspiring book, *Looking Out for Number One*. In it he tells the following story:

> In my early 20s I had the good fortune to be introduced
> to a wealthy old Wall Streeter. A "Wall Streeter" is used here as

an investor who spends each day watching the ticker tape and maneuvering money in and out of stocks at hopefully opportune moments.

Harold Hart epitomized a typical Wall Street success story. Though struggling as a youngster he was now a millionaire many times over. He had it all. The biggie came one evening when I came to visit Mr. Hart to do a deal.

When I arrived I found him resting tranquilly in his favorite chair, with servants waiting on him hand and foot. I sat there awhile waiting as he stared blankly into space.

Finally he muttered, "You know, nature has played a great hoax on man. You work all your life, go through an endless number of struggles, play all the petty little games, and if you're lucky you finally make it to the top. Well I made it a long time ago and you know what? It doesn't mean a damn thing. I tell you nature has made a fool of man and the biggest fool of all is me. Here I sit, in poor health, exhausted from years of playing the game, well aware that time is running out and I keep asking myself, Now what genius? What's your next brilliant move going to be? All that time I spent worrying, maneuvering—it was meaningless. Life is nothing but a big hoax. We think we're so important, but the truth is, we're nothing."

Ringer tells the story because he was convinced that he, unlike the old tycoon, would enjoy his wealth when he accumulated enough to enjoy it. But my money goes on the presumption that he never accumulated enough to enjoy. Enough is never enough. There's always that elusive "something more."

Izaak Walton wrote in *The Compleat Angler*, "There are money-getting men, men that spend all their time in getting and then in anxious care to keep it, men that are condemned to be rich and then are always busy and discontented."

That's the explanation for those busy, discontented men and women we know who use up their entire lives making money. They have more of it than they could ever spend yet they remain driven by an insatiable desire for more. The money means nothing; the game is the thing.

What I mean is this: all our projects—whatever they are—are doomed to failure. Whatever the object of our quest, when we find it we discover that it does not contain the satisfaction we seek.

"Success is an empty bag," Ted Turner said in an interview with Barbara Walters. "But you've got to get there to know it." Emily Dickinson put the same thought another way: "Success is only sweet to those who ne'er succeeded."

"Sweet success" is an oxymoron. Success can only leave us with a ravaging thirst for more and a growing sense of bitterness and despair. We have followed emptiness, Jeremiah says, and we have become empty (Jeremiah 2:5).

There's a reason for that emptiness. God in his infinite love and wisdom has foiled us. He has seen to it that our endeavors fail to satisfy us because he loves us too much to let us go. He will deny us and thwart us until there is nothing left but God. "He threatens terrible things," George MacDonald says, "if we will not be happy."

Perhaps you're a cistern-digger, driven by soul-thirst. Only God can satisfy your heart. Everything else will deceive and disappoint.

But Jeremiah paints another picture: a "spring of living water" (Jeremiah 2:13), rising from hidden depths, pouring into our hearts, satisfying us even as it makes us thirst for more, always flowing in abundance, always accessible.

There's a river of God's love flowing at your feet. Put down your pick and shovel. Stoop down and drink. "Whoever is thirsty, let him come; and whoever wishes, let him take the free gift of the water of life" (Revelation 22:17).

In C. S. Lewis's *The Silver Chair*, Jill finds herself transported into a strange land because of her own pride and foolishness. She is lost and very thirsty, and looking for a stream. She finds a brook, but she also finds the Lion, Aslan, a symbol of Jesus, lying beside it. Aslan growls and tells her she may come and drink.

> "May I . . . could I . . . would you mind going away while I drink," said Jill.
>
> The Lion answered with a look and a very low growl and as Jill gazed at its motionless bulk, she realized that she might as well have asked the whole mountain to move aside for her convenience. The delicious rippling noise of the stream was driving her nearly frantic.

"Do you promise not to—do anything to me if I do come?" said Jill.

"I make no promise," said the Lion.

Jill was so thirsty now that, without noticing it, she had come a step nearer.

"Do you eat girls?" she said.

"I have swallowed up girls and boys, women and men, kings and emperors, cities and realms," said the Lion.

It didn't say this as if it were boasting, nor as if it were sorry, nor as if it were angry. It just said it.

"I daren't come and drink," said Jill.

"Then you will die of thirst," said the Lion.

"Oh, dear!" said Jill, coming another step nearer. "I suppose I must go and look for another stream then."

"There is no other stream," said the Lion.

CHAPTER 5 | A MAN OF FEW WORDS

Where can the Word be found?
Not here. There is not enough silence.

—T. S. Eliot

READ Psalm 39

IT'S WISE TO BE BRIEF, TO SAY AS LITTLE AS POSSIBLE TO OTHERS and as much as possible to God. "Many words are meaningless," says the wise man (Ecclesiastes 5:7). Too much talk weakens our character. It's like the continuous running of a faucet that empties a well. Talking leaves no time to commune with ourselves and with God.

"Silence is the mother of the wisest thoughts," said Diadochus, an early Christian writer. Our thoughts mature in quiet moments. If we're always talking, we give no opportunity for our hearts to receive the promptings of the

Spirit; we can't hear what others are saying and we can't hear what the Spirit wants us to say.

Furthermore, we can't be talking all the time without saying things that cause us regret. We talk too much about ourselves or too much about others. Our words coerce, contaminate, and offend our friends.

How often have I walked away from meetings with a bad taste in my mouth (could it be my foot?), thinking, "I should have left some things unsaid."

> Why is it that so often I return
> From social converse with a spirit worn,
> A lack, a disappointment—even a sting
> Of shame, as for some low, unworthy thing?
> Because I have not, careful, first of all,
> Set my door wide open, back to the wall,
> Ere I at others' doors did knock and call.
>
> —George MacDonald

"When words are many, sin is not absent" (Proverbs 10:19), a verse which Augustine said "frightens me a great deal." It frightens me a great deal as well.

"Do you see a man who speaks in haste? There is more hope for a fool than for him" (Proverbs 29:20). The one who is hasty—who always has to say something—

usually doesn't consult God at all. He already knows what's best for any situation. He can act on his own. "Such a man," says Fenelon, "is the greatest fool in the world."

How often I have played the fool by being much too chatty. I must learn to be silent before God—set the door of my heart wide open, back to the wall—and ask him to fill me with his words and his wisdom. It's in silence that God will give me something to say. He will teach me to speak—or not to speak.

Isaiah said of our Lord, "He will delight in the fear of the LORD. He will not judge by what he sees with his eyes, or decide by what he hears with his ears" (Isaiah 11:3). Jesus heard and saw many things, but he never uttered a word on his own. He said of himself, "Whatever I say is just what the Father has told me to say" (John 12:50).

When the Pharisees came to Jesus with the woman caught in adultery, he did not reply to their question immediately, but knelt for a moment and scribbled something in the sand. I have no idea what he wrote, but I think I know what he was doing: he was waiting to hear from his Father.

When he finally spoke, he spoke one short sentence: "If any one of you is without sin, let him be the first to throw a stone at her" (John 8:7). Those few words accomplished more than any self-derived sermon would have achieved. Even today those words resound around the world. We must stop and think before we speak, but more to the point, we must stop and pray.

I think of Vincent Van Gogh's painting of a quiet, inviting cottage beside the road. There's a warm fire inside that no one can see, but wisps of smoke come out of the chimney. Someone inside is tending the fire, waiting patiently for the hour when some traveler will come by and sit down, maybe to talk, maybe to stay. Silence toward others, openness toward God enables us to tend that fire.

James says we must be "quick to listen [to what God has to say]" and "slow to speak" (James 1:19). This is not the slowness of ignorance, emptiness, timidity, guilt, or shame. This is the slowness of wisdom born of dwelling quietly with God.

CHAPTER 6 | FOLLOW THROUGH

It troubles me that I am not better.
>   More help, I pray, still more. Thy perfect
>   debtor
I shall be when Thy child I am grown.
My Father, help me—am I not Thine alone?

—DIARY OF AN OLD SOUL

READ Philippians 3:1–16

I READ A STORY SOME TIME AGO ABOUT PHOTOGRAPHER ANSEL Adams, who studied the piano in his early days and showed a remarkable lack of talent. At one recital he set out to play Chopin's F Major Nocturne and sealed his fate.

"In some strange way," he said, "my right hand started off in F-sharp major while my left hand behaved well in F major. I could not bring them together. I went through the entire nocturne with my hands separated by a half-step."

The next day a friend complimented him on his performance: "Well done, Ansel," he said, "You never missed a wrong note."

I know just how Adams must have felt. I often think to myself: if only I could get it together—make one brilliant assault on the powers of evil and overthrow them forever. If only I could take one stand in the face of temptation and resist it so that sins' attractions would fade away. If only there were some cabalistic ceremony, some mystic utterance that would exorcise for all time the demons of lust, fear, pride and greed. If only . . . If only . . . If only . . .

Instead of a quick fix and final perfection, however, I find myself locked in a tedious struggle against bedeviling sins, an arduous ordeal in which resistance seems to make only the slightest impression. Everything I reform soon returns to its old configuration.

I defeat one sin only to find another rising up to assault me. I resist one temptation only to develop more subtle tendencies. I subdue one humiliating behavior only to have it return suddenly and without warning in another mortifying display. Frankly, it does me a lot of good to hear Paul say, of all the sinners in the world, "I am the worst" (1 Timothy 1:15). I always thought it was me.

I used to think that age would rid me of sin, that someday I would simply outgrow it, but that's a fool's dream. The passing years have not done away with sin, but rather have deepened my perception of it. What I once thought of as peccadilloes I now see as perversions. So much of me is yet unconverted.

I see shades of evil in me now that a former knowledge of God failed to reveal: subtle omissions; ungodly attitudes and orientations; hidden areas of self-interest and self-protection; destructive ways of relating to others; defensive ways of covering up; entrenched areas of self-confidence; deep-seated hungers for human approval; tendencies to gain my identity and worth from things other than God. There comes a time, John Bunyan reminds us, when we enter a region along the frontier where "the contrast between the bride and the Bridegroom is heightened and oft-times renewed."

One thing I've learned: It does no good to "should" myself—urge myself to various and sundry abstinences, or exhort myself to hustle more in the hope that I can make holiness happen. As Luther said, "We are conquered if we try conscientiously not to sin." Laying the law on ourselves doesn't work—at least not for very long. Such efforts may have "an appearance of wisdom . . . but they lack any value in restraining sensual indulgence" over the long haul (Colossians 2:23).

The Law *is* good—don't misunderstand me. It can show us where we've gone wrong, but it has no mechanism for overriding our natural tendency to *do* wrong. It was never meant to cure us; it can only make our disobedience seem worse and make us feel even more guilty. Bunyan, in his *Pilgrim's Progress*, personifies the Law as Moses, who greets his followers and beats them with a stick. "I know not how to show mercy," he shouts.

No, it's not exhortations to try harder or do better that I need. What's needed is the power to behave as I already know I should. Walter Brueggerman speaks for all of us when he writes, "I have found myself discovering that mostly I do not need more advice, but strength. I do not need new information, but the courage, freedom, and authorization to act on what I already have been given in the gospel."

So, I ask myself, "What is this 'courage, freedom, and authorization to act on what I have been given in the gospel'? What is the dynamic for change? What can I do to be more like my Lord?"

In the words of a song I vaguely recall—

> I've got the need to,
> I've got the want to,
> I need the *follow through*.

One odd thing about the process is that things usually get worse before they get better. At first, instead of becoming more like Jesus, we're likely to be shown more of our disconformity. Not to worry, however. God only shows us our ungodliness as he gives us the courage to bear the sight of it.

Furthermore, his purpose in exposing us is always good: it's useful for us to see our true character; that way we are driven to hope in God rather than ourselves.

John Newton knew:

> I asked the Lord that I may grow
>   in faith and love and every grace.
> Might more of His salvation know,
>   and seek more earnestly His face.

'Twas He who taught me thus to pray,
  and He I trust has answered prayer,
But it has been in such a way
  as almost drove me to despair.

I thought that in some favored hour,
  at once He'd answer my request,
And by His love's transforming power,
  Subdue my sins and give me rest.

Instead of that He made me feel
  the hidden evils of my heart,
And bade the angry powers of hell
  assault my soul in every part.

Nay, more, with His own hand He seemed
  intent to aggravate my woe,
Crossed all the fair designs I schemed,
  blasted my gourds, and laid me low.

"Lord, why this?" I trembling cried.
  "Wilt Thou pursue this worm to death?"

"This is the way," the Lord replied,
    "I answer prayer for grace and faith."

"These inward trials I employ
    from sin and self to set thee free,
And cross thy schemes of earthly joy
    that thou might find thy all in Me."

God knows us profoundly, and he knows the exact source of our troubles. His hand strikes in unexpected places and leaves nothing uncovered. "As long as the least bit of self-love remains in the secret parts of our heart," Fenelon said, "God will hunt it down, and by some merciful blow, force our selfishness and jealousy out of hiding."

He does so not to curse us, but to cure us—to drive us to him that we might find our all in his care. There's more at stake, you see, than mere holiness. God wants most of all to have our love.

I ask you—those of you who are fathers—would you rather have a child who was struggling and clinging to you in love, or one who had it all together and never gave you the time of day? I think the former description represents more of what our Father's heart longs for. Oh, he will make us good children soon enough, but first of all he wants our affection.

———

Here's the main thing. If we are to be changed at all, it must be God who does the changing. "All virtue," said Augustine, "is a miracle."

Change is God's gift to his children. He wants it for us and it is his nature to give it. George MacDonald asks, "Are you able to worship a God who will give you all the little things he does not care about, but will not give you help to do the things he wants you to do, but which you do not know how to do?" Or as Jesus put it, "If you, then, though you are evil, know how to give good gifts to your children, how much more will your Father in heaven give good gifts to those who *ask* him" (Matthew 7:11).

We must ask God to change us—give him all that's wrong with us and wait for his working.

Oh, there are other things we can do—meditate on his Word and seek his will with a determination to do it; think deeply about ourselves and the underlying causes of our behavior; avoid people and situations that are ruinous to our souls; worship with God's people and look to them for intercession, encouragement, and support. These things work on us to draw us ever more deeply into his heart and into his hands. In the end only he can change us and make us what we were meant to be. "The one who has called you is faithful and *he* will do it!" (1 Thessalonians 5:24).

It's significant to me that almost all verses that categorically promise answers to prayer are associated in some way or another with the fruit of the Spirit. Consider one example: "Ask whatever you wish, and it will be given you. This is to my Father's glory, *that you bear much fruit* (John 15:7–8, emphasis added).

This is not an unequivocal promise that God will answer every prayer we utter, but rather a promise that God will respond to every longing of ours for change—for greater love, joy, peace, patience, kindness, goodness, faithfulness, gentleness and self-control. If we hunger and thirst for holiness and ask him for it he will begin to satisfy us. That's a promise, and, as Bob Dylan used to say, "God don't make promises that he don't keep."

It comes to this: we can try to achieve righteousness on our own, or we can receive it. The one makes us uptight because we're never good enough to satisfy ourselves; the other makes us grateful for any progress we've made.

Are you dissatisfied with yourself? Do you hate your sin and long to do better? Then you are of the same mind with God and you can ask him to bring growth to you, "first the stalk, then the ear, then the full grain in the ear." He is very strong toward those whose hearts are like his (2 Chronicles 16:9). We may despair of ourselves (that, it seems, is inevitable); but we should never despair of God. He is out to mature us.

But we must know this: maturity, when it comes, will come in its own time and way. We want to look over God's shoulder and see how we're doing, chart our progress, put limits on the process, and in other ways direct it. But that is not our business. Our job is to follow the Lord in humility and simplicity and keep ourselves open to what he is doing in and around us. We must give in to him with a humble heart and let him work everything out for us.

When God directs the work he goes straight for the center of what he hates most in us. It may not be the thing we hate—some disgusting habit that annoys others and humiliates us—but rather something we hold most dear.

He may overlook some flaw we despise and concentrate his work instead on other matters we care less about. He may permit some unsavory habit to linger, "loathed and long," to lead us into humility. He may leave trace elements of the old life—"Canaanites" in the land—so he can teach us how to wage holy war (Judges 3:2).

God alone knows what matters need to be addressed and in what order. "The best prayer that a man may offer, he will not say: 'Give me virtue or else,' but 'Lord, give me nothing but what Thou wilt and dost—Lord what and how Thou doest in every detail'" (Meister Eckhart).

Let God do what seems right to him. Press on in the confidence that his processes are adequate to deal with your sin, asking for his help and offering yourself up to his will, content (though never satisfied) until we "take hold of that for which Christ Jesus took hold of [us]" (Philippians 3:12).

T. S. Eliot put it this way:

> Teach us to care and not to care;
> Teach us to sit still,
> Our peace in His will.

Ponder this gracious assurance: "That our God may count you worthy of his calling, and that by his power he may fulfill every good purpose of yours and every act prompted by your faith" (2 Thessalonians 1:11). He has instilled in you the desire to do better. He who prompted the desire is able to fulfill it.

In the meantime, while you wait for his perfect work, don't worry about your failures. Offer up to God all that worries and annoys you and wait for him in peace.

Phyllis McGinley writes, "The wonderful thing about saints is that they were human. They lost their tempers, scolded God, were egotistical or testy or impatient in their turns, made mistakes and regretted them. Still they went on doggedly blundering toward heaven."

So blunder on. Don't dwell on present failings, or on the dead past. Every day has its mishaps and memories of something we should have done or not done. "Never look back" must be our motto. Press on! Though in-process and incomplete we are freely loved, fully forgiven and on our way to glory. Sin may frustrate us for a day, but God's favor goes on forever and on ahead lies perfection. Someday soon we shall see God face to face and we shall be like him—"holy as the Holy One."

"Rivers know this," Winnie the Pooh assures us. "There is no hurry. We shall get there some day."

CHAPTER 7 | ALL SHOOK UP

Right where I am is where I have to be.

—Folk Song

READ Philippians 4:10–13

I AGREE WITH SATCHEL PAIGE: "THE SOCIAL RAMBLE AIN'T RESTFUL." Everyone needs a place of quiet rest.

Carolyn and I have such a place—an old log cabin in the Sawtooths. No television, no newspapers, no telephones, no people, no problems, no deadlines, no demands, nothing that has to be done. George MacDonald got it right, "It's good to have a long nothing-to-do when everything else is done."

I always hate to go back to Boise from that quiet place, because I've learned over the years that homecomings are seldom sweet. Trouble always arrives about the same time as we do. Impending crises loom over us as we hit the highway; anticipated disasters form in our minds as we turn down our street.

"Expect the worst," we say in cold comfort to one another. We know that our thoroughly tranquilized souls will almost certainly be discomposed by some harbinger of bad news. As any returning astronaut will tell you, reentry is a fiery ordeal!

Sometimes the upsets make me want to stay away for good. I get a yen to take early retirement. I sigh with King David, "Oh, that I had the wings of a dove. I would fly away and be at rest—I would flee far away and stay in the desert; I would hurry to my place of shelter, far from the tempest and storm" (Psalm 55:6–8). Running away is a regular fantasy of mine, but I know it won't do. It's not good to be undisturbed.

The prophet Jeremiah had this to say: "Moab has been at rest from youth, like wine left on its dregs, not poured from one jar to another. . . . She tastes as she did, and her aroma is unchanged" (Jeremiah 48:11).

Jeremiah was thinking of the process by which fine wine is made. Grape juice was allowed to stand for a time until fermentation had done its work and the thick sediments had settled to the bottom. The liquid at the top was then drawn off into another vessel. The pouring and settling process was repeated again and again until the wine was fragrant and clear.

God lets us get shook up now and then. Disturbance and disappointment are his discipline: He pours us from jar to jar, keeping us from settling on our dregs.

The unsettling processes of life are bothersome, but they're essential. Rightly understood, they finish our faith: they teach us that the only resting place, as the old hymn has it, is "near to the heart of God."

Dislocations make us more dependent on the peace of God and less dependent on external factors for our tranquility. We become less demanding, less complaining, more willing to let go of what we want. We get sweeter, more mellow, more fragrant, more palatable, more like fine wine.

As always, God has our best interests at heart. Every disappointing, unsettling circumstance of life, every shake-up, has been selected out of all possible options for our highest good. Our present place, no matter how disturbing, is not an accident. It is God's best choice for us. Oh, if only we could see it as God sees it! We would select it as well.

> "Disappointment—His appointment,"
> Change one letter, then I see
> *That the changing of my life*
> *Is God's better choice for me.*
> For, like a loving parent,
> He rejoices when He knows
> That His child accepts, unquestioned,
> All that from His wisdom flows.
>
> —author unknown

CHAPTER 8 | AMALEK AND HIS KIN

We kneel, how weak; we rise, how full of
power!

—ARCHBISHOP TRENCH

READ Exodus 17:8–16

MOSES WAS LEADING ISRAEL UP THE WADI FEREIN TOWARD THE
oasis of Rephidim when Amalek struck from the rear.

Moses later wrote, "Remember what the Amalekites did to you along the
way when you came out of Egypt. When you were weary and worn out, they met
you on your journey and cut off all who were lagging behind" (Deuteronomy
25:17–18).

There is a word for "ambush" in Hebrew, but the word Moses uses, here translated "cut off," is related to a word that means "tail"; it suggests that those who had
fallen behind were picked off and plundered.

Furthermore these stragglers are described as "enfeebled"—the old and infirm. The attack was in character; ancient Caananite documents describe the Amalekites as the *Khabbati*, or "plunderers."

Moses supplies the reason for this cowardly assault: "[Amalek] had no fear of God." Amalek was not motivated by national defense or local considerations. His opposition was cosmic; it was directed against God and his plan to bring salvation to the world; as such his attack is emblematic of all assaults on us by the world, the flesh, and the devil—attempts to thwart the good that God has in mind for all of us.

The Amalekites were the literal and spiritual descendants of the immoral and ungodly Esau, "who for a single meal sold his inheritance rights as the oldest son" (Hebrews 12:16). Esau was that profane man who despised his birthright, his place in the line through which Israel's Messiah would come.

Amalek, like Esau, had no use for God. His hostility was spiritual enmity, a malice that ran in the blood and was heightened by the realization that Israel was moving toward the Promised Land and her spiritual destiny as the people through whom God intended to bless the world.

"Amalek was first among the nations," Balaam said (Numbers 24:20), the first of the Gentile nations to declare war on God and his people; thus he is representative of all attempts to frustrate God's efforts to save us. This was the first of the holy wars chronicled in the *Book of the Wars of the Lord,* a history of the ongoing conflict between the Kingdom of Man and the Kingdom of God, a history that's still being written today (see Numbers 21:14). Amalek would never give up!

Ancient Amalek was no paper tiger. A picture found on a chest in the tomb of King Tutankhamen portrays the heat and fury of a battle between the Egyptians and what are thought to be Amalekites—fierce, bearded, long-haired devils. Their army was equipped with chariots; their weapons were javelins, short swords, and bows.

Israel had no army, no military intelligence, no experienced leadership, few weapons of war. All they had was God, but that was enough. "The Lord is a warrior; the Lord is his name" (Exodus 15:3).

The Lord took an oath against those who dared to raise their hand against those he loved. "I will completely blot out the memory of Amalek from under heaven" (Exodus 17:14). He declared endless war against them. He will strive against those who oppose us until all our enemies are routed. He has taken a solemn vow.

Here is how Amalek's demise began: Joshua took up arms against the enemy and fought him tooth and nail in the valley; Moses took his stand on Jebel Táhúneh, a hill that rises 500 feet or more above Rephidim, and lifted up his shepherd's staff—the rod of God, so called because it represented God's presence and power. "As long as Moses held up his hands, the Israelites were winning, but when he lowered his hands, the Amalekites were winning" (Exodus 17:11).

Moses' up-stretched hands symbolized prayer. Ancient Jewish versions paraphrase the text: "When Moses lifted his hands in *prayer,* the house of Israel prevailed, but when he restrained his hands from *prayer,* the house of Amalek prevailed." Joshua engaged the enemy in the field; Moses' business was prayer.

These two aspects of battle still obtain: we must engage every enemy; but prayer is our essential weapon. When the enemy comes in like a flood, we must reach for the help that comes from that unseen realm that surrounds us.

Behind every human opponent lies the invisible power of darkness. Our struggle is not against flesh and blood, but against the spiritual powers that control them. For that reason, "we do not wage war as the world does. The weapons we fight with are not the weapons of the world. On the contrary, they have divine power to demolish [demonic] strongholds" (2 Corinthians 10:4).

My friend Ray Stedman used to say that life is like a Punch and Judy show. When the puppet-villain puts in an appearance, we can take him out with a club, but what have we accomplished? The man behind the scene will simply place another puppet on the stage and begin to pull the strings once more. Far better to get behind the scenes and take out the puppeteer!

God has supplied us with the means to reach beyond the scenes to the unseen realm of reality. His are not the schemes of human endeavor, but an infinitely more powerful strategy—namely prayer. This is the mechanism that puts the forces of God—a *third* force—on the field, a force for which the enemy has no counter-measures.

The main thing about prayer is to keep at it. Jesus said we "should always pray and not give up" (Luke 18:1). But praying is hard work, much harder than waging war. Our hands begin to droop, and Amalek begins to prevail.

Moses had two sturdy friends who took a stand with him on the hill: "When Moses' hands grew tired, they took a stone and put it under him and he sat on it. Aaron and Hur held his hands up—one on one side, one on the other—so that his hands remained steady till sunset" (Exodus 17:12–13).

Matthew Henry wrote, "Our cause is more or less successful, as our friends are more or less strong in faith, and fervent in prayer. We should be glad of such help. We should not be shy of asking it from others."

Luther agreed: "No man should be alone when he opposes Satan . . . . If the prayer of one doesn't help, the prayer of another will."

> [The enemy's] presence arouses the garrison,
> And all are up in arms, and down on knee,
> Fighting and praying till the foe is gone.
>
> —The Diary of an Old Soul

CHAPTER 9 | CREATED FOR A CRISIS

I was not born
Informed and fearless from the first, but
    shrank
From aught which marked me out from
    men;
I would have lived their life, and died their
    death,
Lost in their ranks, eluding destiny.

—Robert Browning

READ Jeremiah 1:1–10

IN J. R. R. TOLKIEN'S *THE HOBBIT*, FRODO LAMENTS HIS FATE TO THE wizard Gandalf: "Why was I born at a time like this?" Gandalf replies, "You were born *for* a time like this."

So it was for Jeremiah, and so it is for you and me.

It was Jeremiah's lot to minister to a nation that was dying. Pride, envy, wrath, sloth, greed, gluttony, and lust—all the Deadly Sins—were killing its soul. Jeremiah's days were as evil as ours.

But evil days are not all bad. Paul writes, "Be very careful, then, how you live—not as unwise but as wise, making the most of every opportunity, *because the days are evil*" (Ephesians 5:15–16). We read that verse as though Paul is insisting we get busy because the days are short, but that's not what he is saying at all. He's insisting rather that perilous days are times of unparalleled opportunity. Those who know God should buy them up. "Redeem the time; redeem the dream," T. S. Eliot said.

But we respond as Jeremiah did, "I don't know a *thing* (which is exactly what he said). What in the world can *I* do?"

The answer is that God has already done everything that needs to be done: He has planned our usefulness. "We are God's workmanship, created in Christ Jesus to do good works, *which God prepared in advance for us to do*" (Ephesians 2:10, emphasis added). There is a course laid out by our Lord's matchless wisdom and love. All we have to do is follow him and he'll make our path plain.

But here's the surprising thing: not only has God prepared the path for us, but he has also prepared *us* for the path. Listen to Jeremiah: "The word of the LORD came to me, saying, 'Before I formed you in the womb I knew you, before you were born I set you apart; I appointed you as a prophet to the nations'" (Jeremiah 1:4–5).

Before Jeremiah was born, he was known and uniquely crafted for a special task. How this can be consistent with the exercise of free will and choice, I cannot say. That's a mystery. I can only say it's true, and what was true for Jeremiah is true of us as well.

What this means is that at conception God placed in us all the faculties necessary to carry out our unique role in this world. Our bodies, minds, emotions, and wills were formed by him for the particular work for which we've been eternally intended. And then God broke the mold.

Unique purpose has been built into our being and we're endowed with all the special aptitudes which that purpose demands. God has shaped us for our destiny, storing up in us all that he knew would be required for our life-work. There is no condition for which he has not made provision and no faculty which sooner or later will not have its proper exercise and use.

This means that all our abilities are a gift from God to be put to his intended use. A superior intellect, a powerful and well-coordinated body, an engaging personality, a quick wit—all are gifts that make us more useful.

But that also means that our so-called liabilities are part of God's plan. There is a reason for being small, a reason for having a weak voice, a reason for having a battered, damaged body or mind. Our flaws, defects, imperfections, faults and other contradictions are part of the unique creation God imagined, made, and set apart for the particular work he has in mind.

So you're not tall, dark, and handsome. So you're not a bundle of energy and dynamism. So you're not the most scintillating and articulate guy around. No matter. Remember Moses? "O LORD, I have never been eloquent, neither in the past nor since you have spoken to your servant. I am slow of speech and tongue." The LORD said to him, "Who gave man his mouth? . . . Is it not I, the LORD?" (Exodus 4:10–12).

Your limitations are a gift from God and part of his preparation for your work. Through his creative skill and by his ongoing grace your limits can become the means by which God uses you to touch others in singular and uncommon ways. All of which means that you must not despise God's gifts, nor should you desire another's giftedness. Other people's gifts, whatever they are, are not necessary for the work God has called you to do. It's enough for you to know that God has a unique plan for you and that he has made you one-of-a-kind to complete that plan. Remember Peter's question: "Lord, what about him?" (pointing to the apostle John). But Jesus replied, "What is that to you? You must follow me" (John 21:21–22).

Life is necessarily lived piecemeal, and it is difficult, if not impossible, to discern in advance the unique work God has for you. You must know, however, that God *does* have a special work for you to do and that you are God's special creation to implement that work. Søren Kierkegaard said, "Life must be lived forward, but it can only be understood backward."

"But," you ask, "how will I know my work? How will I find that particular purpose for which I'm intended?" Hear what God said to Jeremiah: "Go to everyone I send you to and say whatever I command you" (Jeremiah 1:7–8).

God's call is first a call to follow him in obedience—to go each day where he wants you to go and say what he wants you to say. It is only as you look back over the path of obedience that you'll be able to see what God has been doing with you all along. His plan is always better seen in retrospect than in prospect.

God has called you to a Great Adventure. Follow him in obedience—do the very next thing he asks you to do—and see what happens!

> "Anyone can find out what will happen," Aslan said to the children as he shook his great mane. "Get up at once and follow me. What will happen? There is only one way of finding out."
>
> —C. S. Lewis, *Prince Caspian*

CHAPTER 10 | FOR GOODNESS' SAKE!

All things work together for good!

—THE APOSTLE PAUL

READ Romans 8:18–39

THE WORLD AROUND US SEES NO VALUE IN SUFFERING. PAIN IS blind, bitter, and fruitless—something to be avoided. Ordinary men and women, therefore, will always seek the easier and less costly route.

Not so with God's children. Suffering is not an evil to be avoided, but a call to be embraced: "For it has been granted to you on behalf of Christ not only to believe on him, but also to suffer for him" (Philippians 1:29).

A difficult marriage, a meaningless job, a broken body, a disturbed mind—all are means by which Christlikeness is born in us and begins to grow. Pain moderates our unfaithfulness, irritability, intolerance, greed, and self-centeredness. It rids us of our preoccupation with earth so that we take less interest in it and turn our thoughts to the eternal and invisible.

Though he was a full-fledged Son of God, Jesus, we're told, was made perfect by suffering. We too learn from our suffering, far more than from any other source of learning. "Affliction is the best book in my library," Luther said. Pain completes us. Without it we could never amount to anything.

But suffering has a purpose beyond us. It is for our sake, but it is for God's sake as well. It is the means by which he prepares us for himself, beautifying us so he can enjoy us forever.

The Westminster Catechism states that the chief end of man is "to love God and enjoy him forever," but God would have us know that *his* chief aim is to love *us* and enjoy *us* forever. "The joy of heaven," someone has said, "is not primarily our joy but God's."

There are those Pygmalion stories, like *My Fair Lady,* in which some gracious benefactor finds a miserable young woman, lifts her out of poverty and squalor, beautifies her and gives her new life so he can take delight in her and love her for a time. God does all this for us and more: he lifts us out of our sin and defilement and recreates his image in us, readying us for his eternal kingdom so he can enjoy us *forever.* Eternal love awaits us when all God's work is done.

Browning wrote with remarkable insight of what he called "this changing dance of plastic circumstance . . . machinery meant to give the soul its bent." He sees himself as a lump of clay "bound dizzily" to circumstance's wheel, each whirl forming, shaping, making him until he has been made into a vessel "sufficiently impressed."

"And why?" he asks. Why does God need this rude cup turned out on earth's wheel? We must "look not down, but up," he insists, "for uses of the cup." It is "to slake his [God's] thirst."

To be formed by God for his own lips! To be a vessel to quench *his* thirst! What a stupendous thought! To know that in some inexplicable way God not only wants us, but thirsts for us, yearns for us until his thirst is assuaged. "There is a property in God of thirst and longing" says Julian of Norwich, "he hath longing to have us."

Thus Browning prays—

> So take and use Thy work:
>   Amend what flaws may lurk,
> What strain o' the stuff, what warpings past the aim!
>   My times be in Thy hand!
>   Perfect the cup as planned!
> Let age approve of youth, and death complete the same.

But there is yet another way in which pain serves its purposes: it is also for the sake of others. There is no one better able to enter into others' sufferings than one whose heart has been broken by the rough handling of the years and then bound together by God's sure and healing hands.

You know Paul's words in 2 Corinthians 1:3–6:

> Praise be to the God and Father of our Lord Jesus Christ, the Father of compassion and the God of all comfort, who comforts us in all our troubles, so that we can comfort those in any trouble with the comfort we ourselves have received from God. For just as the sufferings of Christ flow over into our lives, so also through Christ our comfort overflows. If we are distressed, it is for your comfort and salvation; if we are comforted, it is for your comfort, which produces in you patient endurance of the same sufferings we suffer.

Paul, in another place, enumerates his imprisonments, floggings, stonings, shipwrecks, hunger, thirst, and countless other calamities—all of which, he said, only made him a *better* minister of Christ (2 Corinthians 11:23).

Our adversity is for others: it enables us to understand the human heart in ways we could never otherwise understand it. It prepares us to connect with the deeper needs of those around us and to give counsel on a level we could never otherwise give. It enables us to teach, guide, soothe, and comfort human souls with great mercy and understanding.

Can it be that our suffering is for the sake of one(s) who caused it? Can it be that a difficult colleague, a rebellious teenager, an aging, complaining parent, an uncaring spouse is the very one for whose sake we are being prepared?

F. B. Meyer once confided to a friend that he felt welcome in any home in England except his own. His loveless marriage was a source of deep misery and heartache, yet Meyer believed that he, by his aching soul, was being prepared to give love and strength to his wife at the end of her days. He wrote to her—

> If then your future life should need
>   A strength my love can only gain
> Through suffering—or my heart be freed
>   Only by sorrow from some stain,
> Then you shall give, and I will take
>   This crown of fire for Love's dear sake.

And so I pray, "Lord, you are the potter; I am the clay. Make me whatever you want and do it by whatever process you choose. Only let me be a vessel that you can enjoy and use forever."

I will submit to obscurity and neglect for your sake if it will make me more like you. I will be overlooked and forgotten if I can be eternally surrounded by your love. I will be counted with Paul as "the scum of the earth, the refuse of the world" if I can be useful in your hands.

I will lie quietly on the wheel as you probe and pound the clay to make it more pliant and tractable. I will pass through the fire of your kiln. Only let me be a vessel of honor, the one you choose and use, always in your hand to be lifted to your lips or the lips of those you love.

Oh, to be so shaped—for ourselves, for God, for others—a vessel formed "for noble purposes, made holy, useful to the Master and prepared to do any good work" (2 Timothy 2:21).

CHAPTER 11 | SAGE AND HOLY MELANCHOLY

But hail thou Goddes, sage and holy,
Hail divinest Melancholy.

—JOHN MILTON

READ John 12:24–26

I KNOW MELANCHOLY. I'VE HAD MY BLUE MONDAYS AND MY DARK weeks. Oh, I enjoy long periods of heart-easing joy, but some mornings, for some reason, I find myself under a cloud.

I have a psychiatrist friend who tells me that depression is usually the result of one of three factors: *loss, anger,* or *guilt.* I've often worked through his sources to find the root of my own gloom.

Loss is an inevitable part of life. We lose things all the time—keys, contact lenses, important papers and letters, lunker trout. Most of our losses are minor in the larger scheme of things.

Other losses, however, are catastrophic—death, cancer, rape, abuse take something from us that can never be replaced. One writer observed that while ordinary loss is like a broken arm, catastrophic loss is like an amputation: something is gone forever. Time does not heal all wounds.

Great sadness comes from catastrophic loss and the root of that sorrow, it seems to me, is wanting something that we cannot have. At the risk of sounding indifferent and uncaring, the only way to deal with it is to let go of what you want but cannot have—to die to your right to enjoy good health, good friends, a trouble-free family environment, unconditional marital love, and golden retirement years. Dying is the only way to come alive.

Paul put it this way, "We always carry around in our body the death [or "dying"] of Jesus, so that the life of Jesus may also be revealed in our body. For we who are alive are always being given over to death for Jesus' sake, so that his life may be revealed in our mortal body" (2 Corinthians 4:10–11).

Paul's phrase, "given over to death," refers to those losses and bereavements that cause us such deep sorrow. His answer is to "carry around in our body the [dying] of Jesus," in other words, to adopt the attitude that Jesus brought to every loss: a willingness to give up what he wanted and submit to his Father's will: "Your way not mine."

Jesus died every day of his life. The cross was simply the culmination of a lifetime of dying—to his dreams, his reputation, his career, his friends, his comfort, and eventually to his own life. Every day he gave up something he couldn't have. And so must we. "Die before you die," C. S. Lewis said, "there is no chance after."

Dying is hard. It was hard for Jesus and it's hard for us, yet it is the means by which we know joy again—a greater joy than ever before. In fact, as I think about it, I wonder if we can ever know real joy until we have known profound loss, until all other sources of happiness have been eliminated by earthly sorrow and we have come to Jesus, that tireless lover of our souls. He alone is the source of eternal consolation and joy. In him we know an enjoyment not based on having what we want, but on having *him.* To be without is an indispensable part of happiness—a happiness that "summer cannot wither and winter cannot chill." That's the enjoyment Habakkuk describes:

> Though the fig tree does not bud and there are no grapes on the vines, though the olive crop fails and the fields produce no food, though there are no sheep in the pen and no cattle in the stalls, yet I will rejoice in the LORD, I will be joyful in God my Savior (3:17–18).

Anger is another element that contributes to our gloom. Much has been written about the effect of rage, resentment, mistrust, hate, and suspicion on our peace of mind. All create unrest and depression.

Anger grows out of disappointment and hurt when our needs are not met. Our hurt becomes rage and resentment, and then revenge—the desire to hurt back. There is no peace that way. The anger turns inward on us and crumples our souls. The inevitable result is depression.

Again, recovery means dying. It's a matter of letting go of self-will, of letting God do what he has purposed to do. It does not say, "Give me my rights!" but rather "Lord, give me nothing but what you want"—like Isaac lying passively in the arms of his father, Abraham; like Mary consenting to her humiliation ("Let it be unto me according to your will"); like David acquiescing in his pain ("Let him do to me what seems best to him").

Then there is *guilt*, that still, small voice that makes us feel still smaller. What's the cure? To try to do better? No, this will only make us worse. The best thing for us is to do what God has been doing all along and forgive our ungodly selves. In a way it involves another kind of dying—putting to death our efforts to justify ourselves and purge our own consciences from sin.

Jesus defended his preoccupation with tax collectors and sinners by saying that he had not come to save the healthy but the sick. Of course we're sick and sinful; of course we've gone wrong. Yet we're forgiven. "Christ died for the *ungodly*" (Romans 5:6).

Our Lord's death, in which we participate by faith, was a death to sin. He paid sin's penalty on the cross and rose again to new life. "The death he died, he died to sin once for all; but the life he lives, he lives to God" (Romans 6:10).

Because we are identified with Christ in his death, burial, and resurrection, we too have new life. "The old has gone; the new has come!" (2 Corinthians 5:17). The old "sin question" has been settled. We will sin, but we are free from sin's consequences—its guilt, pollution, humiliation, and bondage.

There will always be acts to regret, apologies to make, mistakes that can never be corrected. There is, however, "no condemnation for those who are in Christ Jesus" (Romans 8:1), which means, among other things, that God does more than rid us of the *feelings* of guilt; he rids us of guilt itself!

We don't have to grieve any longer for anything we've said or done; we do not have to wallow in self-pity. We can confess our sins and move on.

At times it's hard for me to get that forgiveness out of my head and into my heart. The only way I know is to ask for it. Prayer is the means by which we translate truth into reality. There is no other way.

Loss, anger, and guilt all result in sorrow, but it seems to me there may be another element that contributes to it—one not understood by once-born men and women. It may be that our heartache is nothing more than homesickness.

Broken homes, broken relationships, broken promises, broken bodies all remind us that this world is not our home. Heaven lies ahead and there will always be some sorrow in us until we get there. Then (and only then), will God "wipe every tear from (our) eyes" (Revelation 21:4).

Finally, it has come to me in recent years that our dark moods, for all their aching discomfort, are in fact a grace disguised, for, whatever their cause, they can become the means by which God draws us into prayer and contemplation and thus into deep understanding. Blue is "staid wisdom's hue."

It's best to accept our gloom when it arrives, for steadfastly borne it can push us closer to God and give us more of the wisdom that comes from above.

And may at last my weary age
Find out the peacefull hermitage, . . .
Till old experience do attain
To something like Prophetic strain.
These pleasures *Melancholy* give,
And I with thee will choose to live.

—John Milton

CHAPTER 12 | THE DISCIPLINE OF DELAY

So often we mistake God and interpret his
delays as denials. What a chapter might be
written of God's delays. It is the mystery of
educating human spirits to the finest temper
of which they are capable.

—F. B. MEYER

READ Numbers 9:15–23

I WATCH THE THUNDERHEADS MASS AND BILLOW OVER THE BOISE
Front and think of "the cloud"—the symbol of the Presence in Israel's midst and
the means by which God's people were led through the wilderness.

Moses had this to say about the cloud: "Sometimes the cloud was over the
tabernacle only a few days" (Numbers 9:20); other times the cloud "remained

over the tabernacle a long time" (9:19)—several days, a month, a year—and God's people waited and waited and waited.

Waiting is hard. We twiddle our thumbs, shuffle our feet, stifle our yawns, and fret inwardly in frustration. We want to hit the road.

"Ah, for the open road," sighs Mr. Toad. "There's the real life for you . . . . Here today and off somewhere else tomorrow! Travel, change, interest, excitement! The whole world before you, and a horizon that's always changing."

Like Toady, we want to put miles behind us, see new sights. Change, interest, excitement! That's the life! But the cloud lingers and so do we. We feel trapped by drab routine, day in and day out duty, the monotonous grind, the same ol', same ol'.

We writhe under our frustration and helplessness.

"This is no place to grow," we complain. "What chance do I have to develop my full potential? What opportunity do I have to accomplish great things?"

"Haven't I endured enough?" we ask. "Haven't I learned the lesson of this place?"

"Isn't it time to move on?"

"No," is often the answer. The cloud lingers and we make no progress at all— or so it seems to us.

But what seems so is not what is so. Waiting is not an interruption of our journey but an essential part of it. Without delay we could never make the most of our lives. It's one of the ways God effects the ends on which he has set his heart.

F. B. Meyer writes, "Out of myriads of circumstances God has chosen the lot of each as being specially adapted to develop the hidden qualities and idiosyncrasies of the soul He loves. Anything else than the life which you are called to live would fail in giving scope for the evolution of properties of your nature, which are known only to God, as the colors and fragrance which lie enfolded in some tropic seed."

Waiting is the time for soul-making, the time to develop the quieter virtues—submission, humility, patience, endurance, persistence. The quiet virtues take the longest to learn, are the last to be learned, and, it seems, can only be learned through God's delays, the very thing we're most inclined to resist.

We mustn't resist and we mustn't grow restless. We must wait before we make a change by some rash and willful act—before we give notice to a difficult employer, before we walk out on a hard marriage, before we trash a disappointing friendship, or make some other irrevocable decision. We must wait to make the next move. We'll know when it's time to go. God will make the change in plenty of time.

In the meantime we should look into each delay for its disciplines, learning its deeper lessons of faith and obedience and yielding to God's efforts to change *us* rather than our circumstances. The extent to which we do so will determine the extent to which his purposes are achieved in us, or are thwarted.

Meyer writes, "What a chapter might be written of God's delays. It is the mystery of educating human spirits to the finest temper of which they are capable.

What searchings of the heart, what analyzings of motives, what testings of the Word of God, what upliftings of the soul . . . . All these are associated with these weary days of waiting which are, nevertheless, big with spiritual destiny."

CHAPTER 13 | HOW TO READ THE BIBLE

The words of the Lord are seed sown in our
hearts by the sower. They have to fall into
our hearts to grow. Meditation and prayer
must water them and obedience keep them
in the light. Thus they will bear fruit for the
Lord's gathering.

—GEORGE MACDONALD

READ Luke 8:16–18

THERE IS A CRYPTIC SIDE TO GOD: HE DELIGHTS TO HIDE THINGS.
We establish our sincerity and nobility by looking for them. "It is the glory of
God to conceal a matter," says the wise man; "to search out a matter is the glory
of kings" (Proverbs 25:2).

The incarnation is a good example of this encoding: God hid himself in a human being. There was nothing on the surface that would have made Jesus recognizable as God. Only those who searched him out, sat at his feet, and followed him in obedience ever found out who he was.

In the Upper Room, in answer to the anxious question of Judas (not Iscariot) about why Jesus would only manifest himself to his friends, Jesus replied, "Whoever has my commands and obeys them, he is the one who loves me. He who loves me will be loved by my Father, and I too will love him and show myself to him. . . . If anyone loves me, he will obey my teaching. My Father will love him, and we will come to him and make our home with him" (John 14:21, 23).

So it is today. God hides himself in his Word and reveals himself to those who *love* him. As it is written: "No eye has seen, no ear has heard, no mind has conceived what God has prepared for those who love him" (1 Corinthians 2:9).

Jesus put the same idea another way:

> For there is nothing hidden that will not be disclosed, and nothing concealed that will not be known or brought out into the open. Therefore consider carefully how you listen. Whoever has will be given more; whoever does not have, even what he thinks he has will be taken from him (Luke 8:17–18).

There are two groups envisioned here: the "haves" and "have-nots." The "haves" are those who have soft and submissive hearts. They will be given more knowledge—move "further up and further in." The "have-nots" are those who have hardened their hearts. What knowledge they once had is taken away. The truth fades into forgetfulness.

If we do not want God he will not foist himself on us. To do so would trivialize his Word and brutalize us. Unlived truth hardens the heart and breeds contempt. For us to know more when we will not live it is our worst judgment.

So God in his love takes his Word away; he sends a famine—"not a famine of food . . . but a famine of hearing the words of the LORD" (Amos 8:11). We read the Bible, but we get nothing from it. We study it, but we go away empty-handed and confused.

George MacDonald writes:

> What (the biblical writers) care about is plain enough to the true heart, however it is far from plain to the man whose desire to understand goes ahead of his obedience . . . . He who does that which he sees, shall understand; he who is set upon understanding rather than doing, shall go on stumbling and mistaking and speaking foolishness. It is he that runneth that shall read, and no other.

These days so many approach the Word purely as an object of intellectual pursuit, as though truth can be known by the mind alone. But the more we pursue God in this way, the more distant he becomes. Then terrible things begin to happen to us: knowledge takes the place of wisdom; hubris takes the place of humility. The process breaks down into positions, disagreements, and intellectual pride.

Truth cannot be known through the intellect; it must be known through the heart. The more we love God and obey him the more we know. Only love makes God real and brings him to us. That's the biblical theory of knowledge, a way of knowing that is hidden from the wise and prudent and given to babes.

It seems to me that those of us who take the Bible straight are more inclined toward explanations than we are toward obedience. First we must understand the Bible, we say, and then we'll do it.

Truth does call for explanation, but not as much as we think or as much as we want. There is an order in the way God reveals himself, and that order is inviolate: he speaks; we obey; he explains it—maybe. It's simply not true that God must explain everything to us before we can obey him. He's not obligated to explain anything to us, and some things he can't explain until we get to heaven and have his pure heart.

More than a hundred years ago, revivalist Charles Finney issued a caution about trying to understand everything before we set out to obey. This practice, he said, would inevitably produce a critical, intellectual pride, that "either has no real faith or holds most loosely to Divine things that do not admit of a clear explanation." In other words, if I don't understand a particular text I don't have to do what it tells me to do.

But Scripture teaches us that we must obey God's Word whether we understand it or not. We must bow before each word in humble submission. As T. S. Eliot taught us,

> You are not here to verify,
> Instruct yourself, or inform curiosity
> Or carry report. You are here to kneel.

When we kneel in worship and submission, then and only then do we begin to see. "Obedience," Tozer says, "is the opener of the eyes."

As you read a passage from the Scriptures, pause after each verse or phrase to hear what God is saying to you. Consider how to practice what you've read. Think about how other believers may have lived out this truth. Consider what may keep you from living out the truth yourself.

As you sense your inability to obey some truth, come before God humbly and tell him how helpless you are. Ask him to live his life in you and to do all that you cannot do. He will finish the work that he has called you to do.

Sometimes I speak to men who tell me they don't understand the Bible. They're looking for a method that will shed more light on the text.

I rarely suggest a method, though there are many, because methodology is hardly ever the issue. I rather remind these men of something Peter said: "Rid yourselves of all malice and all deceit, hypocrisy, envy, and slander of every kind. Like newborn babies, crave pure spiritual milk, so that by it you may grow up in your salvation" (1 Peter 2:1–2).

Peter's analogy is easy to follow: hunger is a natural condition for healthy children. It's sickness that takes away their appetite. If we obey what we already know of God's Word—rid ourselves of the pathogens of malice, deceit, hypocrisy, envy, and slander—we will understand what we have read and we will develop a hunger for more.

If you find confusion in your mind, it may be that there's some evil thing in your heart, some unrepaired wrong. "Those who by insincerity and falsehood close their deeper eyes are incapable of using the more superficial eyes of their understanding," George MacDonald said.

What's the solution? Read the Word with your heart wide open. Let God speak to the insincerity and subterfuge in you. Let him prove and delve into your pride, avarice, greed, hateful thoughts, resentful grudges, indifference to human need. Let him disinter every buried secret and reveal every dark thought. Permit him to speak to every harmful habit, every bad attitude, every troubling perspective, every destructive way of relating to others. "Let there be no delay," John Wesley said. "Whatever you resolve begin to execute the first moment you can."

But here I must issue a caution: seek the will of God with a resolution to do it, but seek to do it through his grace alone. Grace is the operative word. It is grace and grace alone that "teaches us to say 'No' to ungodliness and worldly passions, and to live self-controlled, upright and godly lives in this present age" (Titus 2:12). Obedience, to the extent that any of us obey, is God's gift to us.

One thing more: when you get understanding, be sure to give it away as soon as possible. Otherwise it will go to your head.

> In holy things may be unholy greed:
> Thou giv'st a glimpse of many a lovely thing,
> Not to be stored up for us in any mind,
> But only for the present spiritual need.
> The holiest bread, if hoarded, soon will breed
> The mammon-moth, the having pride.

—The Diary of an Old Soul

CHAPTER 14 | THE HOLE IN THE WALL GANG

I have my own four walls.

—THOMAS CARLYLE

READ Ezekiel 8:1–13

THE PROPHET EZEKIEL WAS SWEPT AWAY IN A VISION, TRANSPORTED to Jerusalem to the temple, to the gate through which God's people came to worship. And there, in the entry to the court stood a vulgar, indecent idol described literally as "an idol that makes God jealous."

The idol Ezekiel saw was a phallic symbol, a carved pillar representing the worship of sex and everything associated with it. It stood opposite the Shekinah, the cloud that represented the presence of God among his people.

These forces still vie for our affection. On the one hand there is sexuality; on the other hand, spirituality—the two most powerful forces in the world. The thrill of lust always leads us away from God. Lust and love for God cannot co-exist. They are antagonistic; one displaces the other.

Every day we move between these two passions; every day we're forced to choose whom we'll serve: God or Phallus? The choice we make is the choice we take with us into our souls.

If we bow before God, he will begin to deal with all our other choices. If we worship sex, it will enter into the secret places in our lives and corrupt us. We will go from bad to worse. As the angel said to Ezekiel, in effect, "You haven't seen anything yet!" (8:6).

Ezekiel was taken then to the entrance of the inner court where he discovered a hole in the wall, as though someone had been trying to gain entrance. He was told to start digging—and there he discovered a secret door.

God said, "Go in and see what they're doing in there." So Ezekiel peeked into the room.

First he saw dirty pictures scrawled all over the walls, like the graffiti you see on cubicle walls in public restrooms. Then he saw a group of men on their knees worshiping the drawings on the walls and saying to themselves, "The LORD does not see us" (8:12).

The Lord said to Ezekiel, "Have you seen what the elders of the house of Israel are doing in the darkness, each at the shrine of his own idol?" (8:12), using a word for *idol* that is often translated "imaginations" in the Old Testament.

Imagination is the image-making function of our minds, the remarkable ability we have to form mental images with thoughts even though actual objects are out of sight. It's a promising faculty, but one we can prostitute, making the pictures pornographic, playing at sex in our heads, bedding down in that secret boudoir in our brain.

The first images tend to be ill-defined, but we have the capacity to sharpen the focus and portray the pictures in vivid color and live action on the walls of our minds. Then they become memories, indelibly inscribed drawings to which we return again and again for worship. With each visit the pictures gain greater definition. All this goes on in those secret places from which we have excluded God.

Sexual fantasies are sins we readily excuse. Who knows, who cares, and who gets hurt? A victimless crime—or so we think. But sin always bears bitter fruit in us and in others. We cannot long contain its effects; it always breaks out in greater defilement. As the angel said again to Ezekiel, "You will see them doing things that are even more detestable!" (8:13). The result, as Ezekiel went on to see, is a slow sort of dying.

There is deliverance from this. We must choose whether we'll serve God or Phallus. It's a choice we make every day.

And then we must invite God into every part of our life, even into those darkened rooms in our minds where we have our own four walls—rooms which we have staked out for ourselves, and from which we have excluded him. He will enter in, the entrance of his words will give light, the images on the walls will begin to fade, and he will write his own thoughts in their place. Our love for him will be restored and we will once again be the men God has created us to be.

CHAPTER 15 | JACOB'S LADDER

What doth the ladder mean
Sent down from the Most High?
Fasten'd to earth its foot is seen
Its summit in the sky.

—CHARLES WESLEY

READ Genesis 28:10–22

JACOB WAS ON THE RUN, FLEEING FROM HIS BROTHER ESAU'S FURY, a lonely, frightened fugitive, far from his family home, so lost that even God couldn't find him—or so he thought.

Cold and weary, he came to "no particular place," as the text puts it, and, because night was falling, he cleared a spot in the rubble-strewn ground, rolled out his sleeping bag, found a rock to put under his head, and lay down. "In all his solitude and grief," poet Henry Vaughn writes, "on stones did sleep and found but cold relief."

In his misery and exhaustion, Jacob soon fell into a deep sleep in which he began to dream. In his dream he saw a stairway, rising from the stone at his head, connecting heaven and earth.

The traditional ladder is such an old favorite it's a shame to give it up, but the mental picture of angels scrambling up and down a ladder leaves something to be desired. The term usually translated "ladder" actually suggests some sort of stairway, and it was more likely a stone ramp leading up to the top of a ziggurat.

The ziggurats of that day were equipped with flights of stairs leading up to the summit. Jacob would have been familiar with the architecture. Here's another example of God's passion to communicate, using human metaphors to bridge the gap between the seen and unseen worlds, moving from the known to the unknown.

Ziggurats were normally built alongside a smaller temple on the ground. The lower temple was intended to be a place for mere mortals to gather; the summit of the ziggurat was the place where the gods were supposed to dwell.

The ziggurat, with its steep stairway, was essentially a symbol of man's efforts to plod his way up to God. To get in touch with him, a man had to trudge up a long flight of stairs. It was hard work, but there was no other way (see Genesis 11:1–4).

It's odd how that pagan notion has found its way into our theology and thinking. Early Christian writers used the ladder as a metaphor for spiritual progress, tracing the steps of Christian faith, beginning with the fear of God and moving through obedience and perseverance to the twelfth degree and the summit: "humility and charity which is perfect and casts out all fear." Walter Hilton's literary classic, *The Ladder of Perfection*, is based on that understanding.

The idea is still around. The old camp-meeting song, "We Are Climbing Jacob's Ladder," draws on the same association. In each case the emphasis is placed on the ascent of man.

What caught Jacob's attention, however, was not the stair and the need to ascend it, but the fact that God was standing "beside" him. The phrase everywhere in Genesis means God standing *alongside* (Genesis 18:2 and 45:1).

God had come *down* the stairway. That's the point of the dream. Yahweh himself was present in this strange place, contrary to Jacob's expectations, and far from the holy places Jacob normally associated with God's presence.

"Surely the LORD is in *this place,* and I was not aware of it," Jacob declared with wide-eyed, childlike amazement. "This [place] is none other than the house of God; *this* [stairway] is the gate of heaven."

Jacob got the message of the metaphor, but God was taking no chances. He illuminated the picture with a promise: "*I am with you* and will watch over you wherever you go . . . . *I will not leave you* until I have done what I have promised you" (Genesis 28:15, emphasis added). This was the good word that quelled Jacob's anxiety and lifted his heavy heart.

The narrator then relates how Jacob, very early the next morning, "took the stone he had placed under his head and set it up as a pillar and poured oil on top of it" (Genesis 28:18). In ancient fashion, Jacob upended the stone on which he had rested, poured oil over it, and consecrated the place, naming it *Beth-el,* the House of God.

Then Jacob made a vow: "If God will be with me and will watch over me on this journey I am taking and will give me food to eat and clothes to wear so that I return safely to my father's house, and if the Lord will be my God, then this stone that I have set up as a pillar will be God's house, and of all that you give me I will give you a tenth" (Genesis 28:20–22, my translation).

Jacob is not betraying a grasping, mercenary spirit, bargaining with God for food and drink and then saying, "*If* I get these things *then* Yahweh will be my God." The phrase "then the Lord will be my God" is actually part of a string of conditional clauses and should be translated similarly, "*if* Yahweh indeed is my God . . . ." He is paraphrasing the promise: "I will be with you."

"*Then* . . . this stone . . . will be God's house." In other words, if God indeed stayed with Jacob wherever he wandered, he would return and build on this place an enduring monument to this moment.

Jacob had no idea what lay ahead. His years in Haran would be brutal and painful, filled with anxiety and grief, yet God proved to be as good as his word. He was with Jacob every step of the way. That's what rendered Jacob quiet and at ease despite the difficulties of those days.

Some years later Jacob came back to Bethel and built an altar there to the One who, as he said, "has been with me wherever I have gone" (Genesis 35:3).

Jacob's dream recalls Jesus' words to Nathaniel, that honest and open-hearted Israelite, "You shall see heaven open, and the angels of God ascending and descending on the Son of Man" (John 1:51).

"Son of Man" was Jesus' title for himself—man as he was meant to be. Jesus was the perfect embodiment of the truth Jacob learned at Bethel. He lived in continual, conscious awareness of his Father's presence. "I am not alone," he said, "for my Father is with me" (John 16:32).

That was the secret of our Lord's rich tranquility and ours. We must learn like our Brother to see him who is invisible and see him everywhere. "From youth we have only one vocation," George MacDonald said, "to grow eyes."

When we know that God is near there is a delightful sense of peace. Our own ambitions and desires begin to be muted; a quiet serenity and security starts to envelop us; foes, fears, afflictions, and doubts begin to recede. It doesn't matter much whether we're well or sick, rich or poor, honored or slandered. We can forebear in every setting and circumstance because we know "the Lord is near" (Philippians 4:5).

G. K. Chesterton was once asked by a reporter what he would say if Jesus were standing behind him. "He is," Chesterton replied with calm assurance.

God's invisible presence is a sober fact, not a figure of speech. He is with us when we're awake or asleep. He is present in our car, in our office, at our workbench, in our classroom, in our bedroom. The Lord is there whether we know it or not. He is there because we are there.

That perception—seeing everywhere the One who is invisible—cannot be gained on our own. It's rather a gift of God given in answer to prayer. So Paul prays, as we must pray for ourselves, that the eyes of our hearts may be enlightened that we may see what otherwise cannot be seen (Ephesians 1:18).

Furthermore it is the natural result of our submission to his will. Humble, self-forgetful obedience to God renders him real. If we regard iniquity in our hearts, if we consistently yield to impurity, if we harbor bitterness, resentment, greed, or grandiosity, we will not see him.

Jesus said, "Whoever has my commands and obeys them, he is the one who loves me. He who loves me will be loved by my Father, and I too will love him and show myself [make myself real] to him" (John 14:21). It is, as Jesus said at another time, the pure in heart who see God.

"What you see," C. S. Lewis wrote, "depends a good deal on where you are standing. It also depends on what sort of person you are."

CHAPTER 16 | IN PRAISE OF WEIRD

> I must admit that the meaning of this [text]
> completely escapes me.
>
> —St. Augustine

READ Psalm 131

CAROLYN WAS TRYING TO HELP SARAH, ONE OF OUR GRAND-daughters, become a little less dogmatic. Unlike Augustine, Sarah is certain about everything.

The issue, as I recall, had something to do with whether the movie *The Lion King* was available as a video. Sarah was sure that it was, and she said so.

Carolyn, trying to set a good example, replied softly, "Sarah, I may be wrong, but I don't think it's out in video yet."

"Yes, Nana," Sarah replied, "You *are* wrong!"

Sarah's assertiveness is kid stuff. She's only six and young enough to be too sure of herself. As we grow up, however, we usually become less certain. Too much of life is beyond our ken.

Paul says, "We know in part" (1 Corinthians 13:9), and I suppose we always will. Even in heaven when perfection has come, the joy of discovery will surely continue. We won't know everything there is to know there; we'll be taught of God and learning—learning better and faster, I assume—going "farther up and farther in" as C. S. Lewis said.

(I once remarked to a friend that we might not have Bibles in heaven because we'll be taught by God himself and won't need them there, to which he replied, "Then what will we Christians have to argue about?")

We have an English word, "weird," that refers to things that are odd or strange. The word is derived from an Old English word, *wyrd,* which meant something a little different. It had to do with things that were unaccountably mysterious and uncanny and better left that way.

We don't allow much *wyrd* these days, at least in the circles I frequent. We have a place for everything and everything is in its place. All things are neat and tidy and tucked away.

I must say, however, that a lot of my certainty has begun to evaporate lately simply because I don't understand as much as I used to. It's not that I lack conviction about the reality of God, but rather I've come to see that in my attempts to explain him I'm mostly in the dark. His ways are "beyond [my] understanding" (Job 36:26).

One of the church fathers, Ireneaus, pointed out that the essential difference between orthodoxy and heresy is that orthodoxy is rooted in paradox and mystery. Heresy, on the other hand, is rooted in clarity and precision. I find a lot of wisdom in those words.

I used to have clear and precise explanations for most things, but when I finally got around to thinking about my explanations, it occurred to me that I really didn't know what I was talking about. I had the right words, but I didn't know what the words meant.

Now I don't know as much as I used to. In fact, as I often say to Carolyn, I find myself believing more and more ardently in fewer and fewer things.

It came to me one day that my mind was much too busy and argumentative to know the peace of God. Always reasoning and worrying—I had no time to cultivate that silence in which God speaks. The main thing for me now is not to know all the answers, but to know God, made real and personal in Jesus. What I hunger for is a purer vision of him through his Word and a greater love for him. Theories about when, where, how and why don't bother me much anymore. Oh, I think about such things from time to time, but they don't hang me up the way they used to.

I like the portrait David paints of himself: "My heart is not proud, O LORD, my eyes are not haughty; I do not concern myself with great matters or things too wonderful for me. But I have stilled and quieted my soul; like a weaned child with its mother, like a weaned child is my soul within me" (Psalm 131:1–2).

This isn't Nirvana's "never mind," but rather the thoughts of a man who has his mind right—no longer restless, searching, craving, struggling with the mysteries of life, but quietly abiding in his Father's love.

I pray often for David's spirit and for the realization that only a few things are necessary—as Jesus put it, "really only *one*" (Luke 10:42 NASB).

"But," a friend of mine once observed, "questions imply answers. If God put questions in our minds, doesn't he have the answers in his?"

Of course he does, but we don't have to have the answers—that's the point. We can live with paradox and mystery. We can know "in part" and be comfortable with not knowing the whole.

"But doesn't God draw lines?" you ask. Indeed he does. He draws straight lines, but they're "pure" lines, as MacDonald said, "without breadth and consequently sometimes invisible to mortal eyes." (MacDonald was thinking here of theological lines. God's *moral* lines are very clear.)

Those lines—theological lines that sometimes divide us—are most often lines that aren't meant to be noticed at all. They're better taken lightly or set aside if we can't see them well.

I often think of this idea—that some of God's lines are drawn invisibly—when I sit down to write one of these essays. It has made me much more reticent when I write and hopefully a little more humble, lest my writings merely add to the sum total of ignorance in this world. That would be a futile achievement.

Theologian Karl Barth imagined entering heaven with a pushcart full of his books and hearing the angels chuckle. "In heaven," he said, "I shall dump even the *Church Dogmatics* [his primary work], over the growth of which the angels have long been amazed, on some heavenly floor as a pile of waste paper."

Furthermore, the fact that I know "in part" affects the way I look at other believers—especially those not exactly like me. Most things about which we disagree don't matter to me anymore.

It occurred to me one day, while reviewing our church doctrinal statement, that our assertions were so inclusive they were exclusive. There were a lot of things there over which Christians have differed for centuries. I wondered why we included them.

Augustine, John Calvin, Martin Luther, and a host of other heroes could not have enjoyed our fellowship. Our creed, which sheltered us so well, would have stifled them.

Our honest desire to think accurately about God can move too easily into a conviction that our doctrinal statements contain everything there is to know about God, which, in turn, has the effect of reducing God to our creed. Without humble uncertainty, our statements can evolve into hard dogma that isolates us from one another. Certainty can breed intolerance. "No one damns like the orthodox," as they say.

Modes of baptism, forms of church government, versions of the Bible, end-time scenarios—issues that have been up for grabs from the beginning—become the main things, the distinctives that divide us physically, emotionally, and spiritually. The whole business makes me sad.

Ruth Bell Graham got it exactly right:

> Why
> argue
> and fight
> and worry
> how the world ends?
>
> Pray for the best,
> prepare for the worst,
> and take whatever God sends.

This understanding has something to say about our efforts to give away our faith. We must, in the midst of our certainty about some things, humbly acknowledge the mystery of all things. We're dealing with matters we don't fully understand; in truth, we know very little about God.

This means we don't have to have all the answers. We can be awed and perplexed. We can be befuddled. We can be at a loss for words. We can say, "I don't understand this, but . . ." We can even be silent.

Donald McCullough, former president of San Francisco Theological Seminary, has said that humility should so encompass our statements about God that we are driven to speak "with the tone of a high school sophomore telling what she knows about vectors to a Nobel prize-winning physicist. What we say may be true enough, but so obviously spoken out of ignorance that we dare not chatter on in blissful confidence. Perhaps," McCullough goes on to say, "it is time for a deferential hush" (*The Trivialization of God*).

Finally, this understanding—that we know very little—has something to say about the way we look at our own growth in grace. The main thing is not to know more things, but to live out the things we know: to love the Lord our God with all our heart, soul and mind and follow him in grateful obedience. We do not need to know the secrets of God. We just need to love him and do what he shows us to do.

Paul, at the end of his life, said that he had only one thought: "to know Christ and the power of his resurrection and the fellowship of sharing in his sufferings, becoming like him in his death" (Philippians 3:10). That just about says it all.

I recall hearing a story about that wonderful old saint, John Newton, whose mind, as he aged, began to fail. "I recall but two things now," he said: "I am a great sinner and my Jesus is a great Savior."

It's a blessing, I think, that we forget most of what we once knew. I can hardly wait for that day.

CHAPTER 17 | THE MAJESTY OF MEEKNESS

[The Lord] knows the true nature of things;
he knows that moderation, not a fierce
defense, beats back a fierce attack.

—JOHN CHRYSOSTOM

READ Romans 12:9–20

MEEKNESS IS NOT LOWLINESS OR HUMILITY. IT'S AN ATTITUDE TAKEN against critics and detractors—not retaliating or returning evil for evil, but bowing in silence and submission before those who do us wrong. It's the opposite of self-assertiveness, but it's also the opposite of weakness. Meekness, as Ray Stedman used to say, is "strength under control." It's stronger than any passion in the world.

Oswald Chambers writes, "To bear with unfailing meekness the spiteful attacks of malice and envy; not to be overcome by evil, but to overcome evil with good; to suffer wrong; to possess one's soul in patience; to keep the mouth with a bridle when the wicked is before us; to pass unruffled and composed through a cyclone of unkindness and misrepresentations—these are those who bear themselves as heroes in the fight."

In biblical terms the meek are those who rely on God's wisdom and power rather than their own. They know that God isn't trying to settle the world's hash and set everything right these days. They know he's permitting evil men and women to have their way and do their worst, waiting patiently for them to come to repentance. They know that in his good time he will vindicate his elect.

I have myself found great comfort in Psalm 37. I turn to it again and again when I'm fretting over the harm someone has done to me:

> Do not fret because of evil men
>> or be envious of those who do wrong;
> for like the grass they will soon wither,
>> like green plants they will soon die away.
> Trust in the Lord and do good;
>> dwell in the land and enjoy safe pasture.
> Delight yourself in the Lord
>> and he will give you the desires of your heart.
> Commit your way to the Lord;
>> trust in him and he will do this:

He will make your righteousness shine like the dawn,
    the justice of your cause like the noonday sun.
Be still before the Lord and wait patiently for him;
    do not fret when men succeed in their ways,
    when they carry out their wicked schemes.
Refrain from anger and turn from wrath;
    do not fret—it leads only to evil.
For evil men will be cut off,
    but those who hope in the Lord will inherit the land.
A little while, and the wicked will be no more;
    though you look for them, they will not be found.
But the meek will inherit the land and enjoy great peace.

                                    (Psalm 37:1–11)

Meekness is the wisdom that inspired and permeated Jesus' life. He was "gentle and riding on a donkey" (Matthew 21:5). He ministered in "meekness and gentleness" (2 Corinthians 10:1). In the end, he offered himself up "like a lamb to the slaughter; and as a sheep before her shearers is silent" (Isaiah 53:7).

Meekness is also the means by which he overcame his opponents: "By meekness and defeat he won the mead and crown. Trod all his foes beneath his feet, by being trodden down" (Samuel Gandy).

John Chrysostom, a fifth-century Christian, has written:

As long as we are sheep, we overcome and, though surrounded by countless wolves, we emerge victorious; but if we turn into wolves, we are overcome, for we lose the shepherd's help. He, after all, feeds the sheep not wolves, and will abandon you if you do not let him show his power in you.

What he says is this: "Do not be upset that, as I send you out among the wolves, I bid you be as sheep and doves. I could have managed things quite differently and sent you, not to suffer evil nor to yield like sheep to the wolves, but to be fiercer than lions. But the way I have chosen is right. It will bring you greater praise and at the same time manifest my power." That is what he told Paul: My grace is enough for you, for in weakness my power is made perfect. "I intend," he says, "to deal in the same way with you." For, when he says, "I am sending you out like sheep," he implies: "But do not therefore lose heart, for I know and am certain that no one will be able to overcome you."

"Meekness ain't natural," a friend of mine said recently, "Rambo, not Jesus, is lord." Indeed meekness isn't natural, not here in Idaho or any other place on the earth. But our Lord asks nothing of us that he was not prepared to do, and he asks nothing of us that he is not prepared to give. Meekness, like every other virtue, is a gift, the work of God's Holy Spirit and not the human will (Ephesians 4:2–6). He will give it to us if we will ask him for it.

We should pray, as George MacDonald prayed, "Make me into a rock which swallows up the waves of wrong in its great caverns and never throws them back to swell the commotion of the angry sea from whence they came."

God never forsakes the one who earnestly seeks his face. Meekness may not come at once, but it will surely come if we will wait for it.

God describes Moses as a "very humble [meek] man, more humble [meek] than anyone else on the face of the earth" (Numbers 12:3). You can't do better than that.

On one occasion, when some folks gathered in rebellion against Moses' leadership, indicting his motives in the process, Moses said absolutely nothing, but simply "fell on his face" (Numbers 16:4).

This is the majesty of meekness and the mark of a man of God—to keep falling on our faces again and again, entrusting our cause to him who judges justly (see 1 Peter 2:23). Those who insist on their rights, who justify and defend themselves, are in constant turmoil. But the meek find rest.

They also find joy. Isaiah insists that the meek "will rejoice in the Lord" (Isaiah 29:19). When we meet unkindness with courtesy and when the injury has passed over us, we will know pure joy—joy because God himself has comforted us; joy because we have acted righteously; joy because we may have turned another away from an evil purpose; joy because God's deliverance is so much better than anything we could do for ourselves. As James has said, "He gives a [*greater*] grace"—greater than anything we could get for ourselves (4:6).

The meek will eventually get what's coming to them, even what others have taken away. "Blessed are the meek," Jesus said, for they alone shall inherit the earth.

CHAPTER 18 | A WORD FOR THE WEARY

Lord speak to me, that I may speak
In living echoes of Thy tone.

—Francis Havergal

READ Isaiah 50:4–10

PEOPLE ARE WEARY—BONE-TIRED AND BUMMED-OUT BY LIFE'S tragedies and necessities. We find ourselves in conversations with these heavy-laden folks and feel at an utter loss to know what to say. How can we speak "the word that sustains the weary"?

Jesus once said to his disciples that they shouldn't worry about what to say or how to say it: "At that time you will be given what to say" he assured them (Matthew 10:19). That's not to say that God fills our minds with thoughts we've never had before, but that he draws from a deep reservoir of accumulated truth the things that he wants us to proclaim.

The Servant of the Lord, our Lord Jesus, had a good word on the matter:

> The Sovereign LORD has given me an instructed tongue,
>   to know the word that sustains the weary.
> He wakens me morning by morning,
>   wakens my ear to listen like one being taught.
> The Sovereign LORD has opened my ears,
>   and I have not been rebellious;
>   I have not drawn back (Isaiah 50:4–5).

What an arresting image! Morning by morning the Lord drew near his Servant, calling him by name, awakening him and inviting him to sit at his feet, giving him his message for each day, preparing him for its duties and demands. Every day our Lord listened "like one being taught."

That's what enabled our Lord to speak such gracious words to those so desperately in need. He knew the source of his wisdom. He said of himself, "I . . . speak just what the Father has taught me" (John 8:28); I am "a man who told you the truth that I heard from God . . ." (John 8:40); "The words you hear are not my own; they belong to the Father . . ." (John 14:24).

And so it is with us. Every morning our Lord's eyes sweep over us, awakening us, inviting us to sit at his feet, to listen like one being taught, to take what words we need for each day. That's how he gives us an instructed tongue; that's how we "know the word that sustains the weary."

Some of the older translations render Isaiah 50:4, "The LORD God hath given me the tongue of the learned" (KJV). The text actually speaks of "the tongue of a *learner*." In later Jewish literature the word came to mean "a disciple." We must be discipled before we can disciple others; we must be taught before we can teach; we must learn before we can ever be "learned."

We'll never have anything worthwhile to say until we start taking in God's words, and there's no better time to take them in than early in the morning. That way we can hear his thoughts before we hear what others have to say.

God speaks to us in solitude. There he whispers his great and eternal secrets in our ears. There we begin to see what only he can see; there we begin to detect the subtle undertones of his voice. Then we have something to say to others. "What I tell you in the dark," Jesus said, "speak in the daylight; what is whispered in your ear, proclaim from the roofs" (Matthew 10:27).

Telling what mere men have told us doesn't have much impact on others. It may circle around the head, but it doesn't touch the heart. The most persuasive words are spoken by those who are taught by God himself. "I will guide him . . . , creating praise on [his] lips," God says (Isaiah 57:18–19). Good words come from within, the final product of God's thoughts planted in our hearts.

The essential thing is to sit at Jesus' feet and learn from him. The more we receive the more we have to give. It's through prayerful, thoughtful Bible reading and quiet meditation that he speaks from his depths to ours. We must stay in his presence until he entrusts us with his word. John Wesley wrote, "I sit down alone—only God is here. In his presence I open, I read his books and what I thus learn, I speak."

Begin each day with a desire to meet with God. Sit down alone. Listen to his word, reflecting on what he has to say to you. Give yourself time for prayerful contemplation until God's heart is revealed and your heart is exposed.

Think of him as your teacher—present and speaking to you, disclosing his mind, emotions and will. Meditate on his words until his mind begins to inform yours, until you know what he knows, feels, wants, enjoys, desires, loves and hates, until his heart becomes yours.

What he tells you to do begin to do. Obedience is always the first step toward learning more. The more you obey the more you will know. Open your ears as the Servant did; don't be rebellious and don't draw back. Let the word dwell in you richly. Ask the Spirit to work his words out through you in winsome, fragrant behavior.

Then ask God for opportunities to give that word away. Don't be ashamed of your limitations. Don't let your confusion over things you don't understand deter you. Don't be dissuaded by those who try to "pluck out your beard." Just look folks straight in the eye and tell them what God has been telling you. Speak without fear. Give them the best you have.

If you have nothing to say, there's only one cure for your ignorance: sit at Jesus' feet and learn from him. "Hide yourself in God," George MacDonald said, "and when you rise before men, speak out of that secret place."

CHAPTER 19 | THE PETER PRINCIPLE

Even when their foolish words they turned
on him,
    He did not his disciples send away;
He knew their hearts were foolish, eyes were
    dim,
    And therefore by his side needs must
      they stay.
Thou wilt not, Lord, send me away from
    thee.
    When I am foolish, make thy cock crow
      grim;
If that is not enough, turn, Lord, and look
    on me.

—GEORGE MACDONALD

READ Luke 22:54–62

Peter was a commercial fisherman, fishing on one of the most dangerous inland seas in the world, the Sea of Galilee. Every day he faced death. Perhaps that is why, like many other men who live on the edge, he had that calm assurance that made you believe in him.

On one occasion, when our Lord was telling his apostles of the trouble that lay ahead, he suggested they buy a sword. The disciples replied, "See, Lord, here are *two* swords" (Luke 22:38).

Peter had one of the swords, we know, but he may have packed *both* of them—slung low on his hips and tied down. Peter was ready to defend his Lord and die if he had to: "Even if *all* fall away," he swore, "I will not!" (Mark 14:29).

When the Roman cohort came to arrest Jesus in the garden, Peter was true to his word. He took on the mob. You have to admire his courage, though arguably his judgment (as well as his marksmanship) left something to be desired.

If you didn't know better, and you were standing there watching Peter at that moment, you might think that this was his finest hour, but it wasn't, as Jesus made clear. Peter's finest hour was actually the hour of his denial. That's where we see the makings of a good man.

Luke gives us an explicit and candid account of Peter's betrayal. He did not try to shield his friend from the shame. Peter wouldn't have wanted him to, because he wanted others to learn the lessons he had learned: that our strengths are more dangerous than our weaknesses, and that our Lord is as gracious in failure as he is in success.

Luke tells us that at Jesus' arrest all his disciples forsook him and fled. "Strike the shepherd, and the sheep will be scattered," as the prophet had predicted (Zechariah 13:7).

Two of the apostles, however, Peter and John, managed to pull themselves together and follow the crowd to Annas's house. John went inside, since he was known by the high priest, but Peter was left outside the gate.

John immediately missed his companion and went looking for him. Discovering Peter lingering outside, John went to the young woman who was in charge of the gate and asked her to admit his friend.

Someone had built a charcoal fire in the middle of the courtyard to fend off the evening chill, and Peter moved toward the warmth of the fire with the crowd gathered around. The group was composed of soldiers and temple officers along with their families and friends, and they were almost certainly talking about the events of the night. Peter stood with them and listened in, warming himself by their fire and enjoying the warmth of the inner circle.

His inclusion, however, was short-lived. The young woman who let him in the door wandered over and recognized him in the flickering light. Luke says she "stared" at him, perhaps surprised to see him with the crowd acting as though he belonged.

If, like John, he had withdrawn into the shadows of the courtyard, she might have left him alone, but to find him near the fire, amiably chatting with Jesus' enemies seemed so incongruous that she blurted out: "This man was with [Jesus]" (Luke 22:56).

Peter was caught off guard. If he had been arrested and dragged before Annas he might have stood his ground, but he hadn't expected this attack—and he buckled. Confused by the girl's statement and the lapse in conversation that followed, Peter blurted out, "Woman, I don't know him" (22:57). This was his first denial.

After this Peter went out into the outer porch, perhaps to get away from the growing hostility of the crowd. At that moment a cock began to crow, signaling the dawn; but the warning was lost on Peter, for there was another young woman standing nearby who spoke to one of her male companions, who in turn said to Peter, "You also are one of them."

"Man," Peter blustered, "I am not!" (22:58). This was his second denial.

An hour went by. Once again Peter was near the fire chatting with those who were gathered and some man, noting his accent, began to say, "Certainly this fellow was with him, for he is a Galilean" (22:59). Others chimed in.

Peter was frightened and began to curse and swear. "I don't know what you're talking about!" he declared and walked away (22:60). Even as he was speaking, the cock crowed again as Jesus had said it would. This was Peter's third denial.

It happened at this moment that Jesus was being led from Annas's house to Caiaphas and must have passed through the courtyard or one of the porches that surrounded the courtyard. He turned and looked at Peter—a lingering look of mingled love and sorrow—and Peter's heart broke.

He ran from Annas's house through the dark streets of Jerusalem, down through the Kidron to Gethsemane—perhaps to the spot where his Lord had knelt in the grass—and there he wept tears of deep repentance. Dear Peter: quick to defend, quick to deny, quick to repent.

Remarkable, isn't it, that Peter could have fallen so easily? His honest, ingenuous nature didn't lend itself to lying, and he wasn't prone to cowardice, but in the face of ridicule he turned into a mass of pudding.

None of the other disciples would have imagined that the "Rock-man" could become such a hapless, blustering coward. How could Peter have fallen apart so completely?

Well, the answer is easy. He did so because he believed too much in himself. Earlier Jesus had warned Peter:

> "Simon, Simon, Satan has asked to sift you as wheat. But I have prayed for you, Simon, that your faith may not fail. And when you have turned back, strengthen your brothers."
>
> But he replied, "Lord, I am ready to go with you to prison and to death." Jesus answered, "I tell you, Peter, before the cock crows today, you will deny three times that you know me" (Luke 22:31–34).

Did Peter mean what he said? Of course he did. He took a solemn vow that he would not deny his master, "Even if *all* [by which he meant all the other apostles] fall away, I will not." Peter was "the little engine that could."

But he couldn't. His grief and weariness, his hunger for approval, his natural instinct to protect himself did him in.

Firm determination is commendable, steadfast commitment is laudable, but self-confidence is deadly, and there's more of that dangerous stuff in us than even the best of us can imagine.

The main thing is to acknowledge that our strength is the worst thing about us. God fears it and so should we. Strong men blunder around and make things difficult for God and for themselves. There's little that God can do with them. It's only the weak who can be made strong and able.

That's why God has to break down our strength. That's why we have to be humiliated. It's the only way. Peter later wrote, "God opposes the proud but gives grace to the humble" (1 Peter 5:5–6). He learned that lesson through the humiliation of his humiliating denials.

Some years ago Carolyn wrote a poem about Peter's failures and her own. It's one of my favorite poems (as she's one of my favorite poets). Carolyn calls it "Peter's Prayer and Mine."

> Lord, I start so strong
>   saying "Anywhere!"
> And I try to war and to defend you
>   with sharpness and steel.
> But Lord, I merely maim and wound;

You alone can heal.
And then, bewildered in the mess,
    I start denying, all confused.

But Lord, that crowing in the night
    has jerked my spirit to attention.

And now I know—You knew it then—
    I'm weak
    inept,
    cowardly,
    betraying,
    dust,
    guilty—just like him.

O Lord, compassionate and healing,
    You prayed then.

And now I turn
    in humble weakness and
        in faith
    to worship You—and then
        to strengthen them.

Hallowed be Thy name!

Here is another lesson to learn from Peter's denial: God walks with us through our failures. "He keeps his foolish disciples close to his side," George MacDonald said, "for he knows we would never learn anything if he shunned us."

Jesus never gave up on Peter. Under the surface and out of sight there was a singular grace that redeemed and restrained Peter's natural willful and wayward life: it was his passionate love for his Master and his profound hunger to obey him.

Sin is not the worst thing in the world. The worst thing in heaven and earth is a cold, hard heart. Peter had many flaws, but a cold heart was not among them. He loved his Lord passionately. "Simon son of John, do you love me?" Jesus asked. "Lord, you know all things; you know that I love you," was Peter's reply (John 21:17).

The other thing about Peter is that he knew he was loved by his Lord. Nothing he did or didn't do could make God love him more; nothing he did or didn't do could make God love him less. He dared to believe in his Lord's forgiving and renewing grace.

The real quality of the soul is revealed, not in the way that it yields to temptation, but in the way that it recovers from failure. Peter knew he could come back to Jesus again and find the forgiveness he needed.

Carolyn pointed out to me one day that perhaps the only difference between Judas and Peter is that Peter never gave up. There is something much worse than failing. It is failing to try again.

"No amount of falls will really undo us," C. S. Lewis said, "if we keep picking ourselves up each time. We shall, of course, be very muddy and tattered children by the time we reach home . . . . The only fatal thing is to lose one's temper and give up."

Man's forgiveness may be true and sweet
Yet he stoops to give it. More complete
Is Love that lays forgiveness at your feet
And pleads with you to raise it.

—Albert Procter

CHAPTER 20 | THE POTTER'S WHEEL

The Potter fashioned the cup
With whirling wheel and hand;
Hour by hour he built it up
To the form that his thought had planned.
'Twas broken and broken again,
Marred by a flaw, a crack, a stain,
    Marred, so he made it again and again;
    Shaped it with joy and labor and pain.

—Annie Johnson Flint

READ Jeremiah 18:1–4

JEREMIAH WAS TOLD THAT GOD HAD A MESSAGE FOR HIM THAT HE could pick up at the potter's shed. So the prophet went down and found a master craftsman sitting at his wheel, fashioning a pot from a lump of clay, rounding it, bending it to the shape his mind had planned.

But the project began to go awry: the material proved too stiff, or a stone or air pocket in the clay caused the pot to be unsuitable, so the potter crushed it into a formless mass again and remade it into another, better pot. This was the word from the Lord.

Simply put, the message is this: God wants to make the most of us, no matter how misshapen, flawed, or stained we may be by the time God gets his hands on us.

Stiff, unyielding material, grains of grit and determination, pockets of pride and resistance may have impaired the Potter's plan to make us true. Nevertheless, God can remake us into something different and entirely new. "One turn of the wheel," Matthew Henry writes, "quite alters the shape of the clay, makes it, unmakes it, new-makes it."

The chips in us, the straw, the stones, the sand—how many times have we resisted God's separating hand, "when he would, but we would not." The damage and loss seem irreparable. But God does not cast us away. If we are willing he will begin anew: he will reshape us, forming us again as it seems best to him. If he cannot do what he intended to do with us at first, he will make something better. It is his way.

Sin and failure may temporarily frustrate God's purposes for us, yet he is never disconcerted or daunted. He can take what remains of our life and make it better than we ever thought possible. He will in time "sanctify [us] through and through . . . ." Faithful is the one who has called us and *he* will do it! (1 Thessalonians 5:24).

Our character is not set in this world; the glaze and firing take place in heaven. As long as there's life in our bodies, we can be shaped, reshaped, and changed. The starting place is to put ourselves back on the wheel and let God get his hands on us.

We must confess that we've marred his vessel and humbly ask him to make us anew, as he remade Jacob, Rahab, Manasseh, David, Peter, John Mark and a host of other spoiled and damaged men and women. "Take me; mold me; make me," is the prayer we must pray. There is no limit to the progress we can make if we will only yield ourselves unreservedly to his will.

It's not always easy to submit to the potter's hands. Sometimes he must probe and delve deeply for the offending object that would mar the beauty of the vessel. Adversity, loss, disappointment, failure, the shift of "plastic circumstance" are the tools God uses to remake us.

But we must remember that every instrument used to form us—painful though it may be—is wielded by a master craftsman's hand. He makes no mistakes. Nothing can be brought against us that is not for our good.

Nothing can hinder God's progress. He has purchased us for himself at great cost and, if we are willing, he will spend the rest of our lives recasting, remolding us into vessels of honor—fit to bear the Potter's seal.

> Thou art making me, I thank thee, Sire.
> What thou hast done and doest thou know'st well,

And I will help thee: gently in thy fire
I will lie burning; on thy potter's-wheel
I will whirl patient, though my brain should reel.
Thy grace shall be enough the grief to quell,
And growing strength perfect through weakness dire.

—George MacDonald

CHAPTER 21 | THE ROD OF GOD

Naked I wait Love's uplifted stroke
My harness piece by piece
Thou has hewn from me
And smitten to my knees
I am defenseless—utterly.

—FRANCIS THOMPSON

READ Hebrews 12:1–13

I READ FRANCIS THOMPSON'S LINES FROM "THE HOUND OF HEAVEN" and think of that weird and irreverent film *Monty Python and the Holy Grail* and that scene on the bridge in which the Black Knight challenges King Arthur to a duel. Arthur, after a brief scuffle, hacks off one of his opponent's arms.

"Just a scratch," the man mutters and resumes the fight. Arthur proceeds to cut off his other arm and then both his legs. Finally, the knight is left standing on his knees shouting at Arthur: "All right. We'll call it a draw!"

The implication of this scene, ridiculous though it is, is profound for me: I think of those times when I, like that stubborn fool, have refused to give in to God when he has brought me to my knees.

But God never takes "No!" for an answer. He fights on—against us because he is for us—until we are willing to lay down our swords and yield our hearts to him with all their dark maladies.

He engages us despite our indifference or resistance in the hope that someday our needs, or at least our tragedies, will awaken us to his love. The alternative is greater darkness and misery.

God's love is good enough to be severe. Severity is his "strange work . . . his alien task" (Isaiah 28:21), yet he must be stern because it is his fatherly duty. He disciplines those he loves; he punishes everyone he accepts as a son. This is Love's pledge.

> Who then devised the torment? Love!
> Love is the unfamiliar Name
> Behind the hands that wove
> The intolerable sheet of flame
> Which human power cannot remove.
> We only live, only suspire
> Consumed by either fire or fire.

—T. S. Eliot

God's discipline is necessary to purify us and ready us for better things. He employs all his skill and art to bring us back to his love. Big disappointments, small successes, shame, loneliness, weary loss of enthusiasm—"the rags, the husks, the hunger-quest drive home the wanderer to the Father's breast" (MacDonald).

It is a caring and loving Father to whom we're being driven. He "disciplines those he loves." He said of David and his descendants, "When he does wrong, I will punish him with the rod of men . . . . But my love will never be taken away from him . . ." (2 Samuel 7:14–15). When undergoing chastisement we must keep this reality fixed in our minds: God has a compassionate, merciful, pitying face.

It may be that you have taken advantage of God's grace, resisting his will and going your own obstinate way. The result has been disaster; he has taken you to the woodshed. Accept the discipline, remembering that God is treating you as a son. Yield in humble and reverent submission. Bear the yoke with patience; don't kick against the goad. As Eli said when he learned of the death of his sons, the tragic consequence of his neglect: "It is the Lord; let him do what seems good to him."

Look beyond the arrogance and cruelty of men and women who hold the rod to the loving hand of your Father. He has allowed you to experience this trouble to draw you back to himself. Set yourself to learn and learn well the lessons of the present discipline.

To confess wrong, to bear patiently the yoke God has placed on your shoulders, to learn the lesson of the rod, though hard and painful, is the path to happiness and glory. "Humble yourselves, therefore, under God's mighty hand," says Peter, "that he may *lift you up* in due time" (1 Peter 5:6, emphasis added).

God disciplines us not to ruin us, but to restore us and lift us higher than ever before. We can look beyond the pain to what it does for us: it is an opportunity to "share in [God's] holiness." "Oh what I owe," Samuel Rutherford wrote, "to the furnace, the file, and the hammer of my Lord Jesus."

Perhaps you're now passing through a time of chastisement and pain; trouble has come into your life because you've been resisting God's love. Do you think you'll never be happy again? Do you think you've gone so far and destroyed so much that not even God can set things right? Take heart in these words: " 'I am with you and will save you,' declares the LORD. 'I will not completely destroy you. I will discipline you but only with *justice*' " (Jeremiah 30:11).

Good judgment lies behind our correction. God corrects, but he does so with great understanding. Though full of zeal to accomplish his purpose he moves according to the dictates of his wisdom. It may seem that God has consumed us until nothing is left, but he knows what he's doing. The discipline is measured and only for a limited time. Afterward there is a bumper crop of joy.

It may be that your harsh and bitter circumstances will not change. God may not restore your health, your wealth, your business, your family. They may be gone in this world. But God can restore your soul. He can set you right and make you more like him than you ever thought possible—"*more* than before" (Ezekiel 36:11).

Greater holiness is always God's goal. His discipline always yields righteousness and peace for those who have been *trained* by it. The important thing is to be trained by it—to give up our resistance, to take the strokes with patience, to let them draw us back to God's great heart so he can "restore [us] to health and heal [our] wounds" (Jeremiah 30:17).

Then he can take the peaceful, gentler path.

> Throw away the rod,
> Throw away Thy wrath:
> O my God,
> Take the gentle path.
>
> For my heart's desire
> Unto thine is bent:
> I aspire
> To a full consent.

—George Herbert

CHAPTER 22 | THE ART OF MAN FISHING

As no man is born an artist, so no man is
born an angler.

—Izaak Walton

READ Luke 5:1–11

OVER THREE HUNDRED YEARS AGO, THOMAS BOSTON, A YOUNG
Scottish fly fisherman, wrote in his diary,

> January 6, 1699—reading in secret, my heart was touched
> with Matthew 4:19, "Follow me and I will make you fishers of
> men." My soul cried out for the accomplishing of that to me,
> and I was very desirous to know how I might follow Christ, so as
> to be a fisher of men, and for my own instruction in that point I
> addressed myself to the consideration of it.

Boston later wrote a booklet entitled "A Soliloquy on the Art of Man Fishing," in which he spelled out his "considerations," based on what he learned from following the Great Angler.

I too am "a brother of the angle," as that good and true fisherman Izaak Walton would say. It's often occurred to me, as I've worked our Idaho trout streams, that fishing for fish is very much like fishing for men and much could be written on the easy and natural correspondence between the two.

But analogy can only take us so far. Boston's way is better—to follow our Lord and learn our tactics from him. We too must linger over his words and deeds, "so as to be a fisher of men." God's ways are always other and better than ours.

One of the stories in the Gospels that I look to in that regard is Luke's report of "The Great Draught of Fishes," as the old versions title it, a story remarkable in its simplicity and yet profound in its shrewd revelation of God's ways.

The story begins early one autumn morning. Jesus was walking along the shore of Lake Gennesaret, as he often did to get away from the stifling atmosphere of the city, and he came upon two fishing-friends from Capernaum, Peter and Andrew, who were cleaning the trash from their seines. These men, experienced commercial fishermen though they were, had fished all night and caught exactly nothing.

As Jesus stood, watching and, I assume, praying for these two men, a crowd began to gather, as they often did in those early days of Jesus' ministry, and they seated themselves on the ground around him awaiting his instruction. Jesus made straight for Peter's boat, asked him to put out from the shore and there, on the forward deck of his boat, began to teach.

His instructions on this occasion were not Luke's concern for he doesn't reveal what Jesus said. He only tells us what Jesus said to Peter after he dismissed the crowd: "Put out into deep water, and let down the nets for a catch" (Luke 5:4).

Simon demurred, "Master, we've worked hard all night and haven't caught anything" (5:5).

I understand. Good fishermen don't appreciate unsolicited advice, no matter how well-intentioned it is. Those I know consider it criticism, generally ignore it, and move off upstream.

Peter was a veteran angler and he understood fishing as few men did. He knew that in the morning fish schooled in the shallows, not in deep water. Furthermore, he knew that other fisherman, consummate cynics that they are, seeing his boat putting out at that hour, laden with nets and preparing to go fishing, would scoff.

But Peter, despite his embarrassment and uncertainty, did exactly what Jesus told him to do. He and his partner, Andrew, put out to sea and let down their nets. When they had done so they "caught such a large number of fish that their nets began to break" (5:6).

You know the rest of the story: "They [Peter and Andrew] signaled their partners [James and John] in the other boat to come and help them, and they came and filled both boats so full they began to sink."

When Simon Peter saw this he fell at Jesus' feet and cried out, "Go away from me, Lord; I am a sinful man," for, as Luke goes on to tell us, "he and all his companions were astonished at the catch of fish they had taken" (5:8).

Then (and only then) Jesus said to Simon, "Don't be afraid; from now on you will catch men" (5:10).

Here's the lesson: the best man fishers in the world are those who don't really know what they're doing. All efforts at communicating the gospel must begin with that certainty.

———

Peter's sin lay in being sure of himself. He knew how to fish. It was his job; he was good at it; he'd been doing it for a long time.

Undeterred by Peter's abilities, Jesus challenged him at the point of his greatest strength and showed him he knew exactly nothing about fishing. He let Peter fail at the very thing he did best so he could learn to succeed at a greater enterprise—fishing for men.

Here is what Ray Stedman said about Peter's failed night of fishing:

> The night of failure was not without its lessons and its benefits. We can do worse than fail. We can succeed and be proud of our success. We can succeed and burn incense to the net. We can

succeed and forget the Hand whose it is to give or to withhold, to kill or to make alive. . . .

Success—yes, even spiritual success—can be a snare and a ruin, while failure can be an unspeakable benefit. Failure is often the only test by which the real worth and quality of a man or woman can be tried. It is in failure that a man begins to think, to wonder whence his failure comes, to look around and seek for the reasons, to put into his work double watchfulness and double energy, and to look upwards to Him who can turn failure into a glorious achievement.

Peter had worked hard all night on his own, without reckoning on the resources of the One who has dominion over "the fish of the sea, all that swim the paths of the seas" (Psalm 8:6–8). This time, when he let down his nets, Jesus issued a call to the schools of fish scattered all over the lake and drew them irresistibly to Peter's boat.

Peter didn't need to read the water or make the right presentation. He didn't need to get himself to the right place at the right time. That was Jesus' business. Peter's waywardness lay in his confident belief that *he* must lure fish to the net and draw them in.

Peter's sin is the sin that plagues us all. We believe that if we can perfect the art of man fishing—get our theology straight, our apologetic persuasive, our patter down pat—men and women, boys and girls will crowd into our nets. But it isn't so.

We know what it's like to fish all night and catch nothing. Again and again we return to shore with our nets empty. But when we enter into partnership with Jesus, when we make ourselves wholly available to him, he will do the rest.

Our business is to stand and wait, alert to be used. If we get ourselves ready our chance will come. God will get us to the right place, to the right person, at the right time, and give us the right things to say.

On the day of Pentecost, though Peter wasn't expecting much, he let down his net and God filled it with three thousand souls (Acts 2:14–41). In the house of Cornelius, Peter had barely put his net into the water when this hard-living, unlikely pagan jumped in (Acts 10:23–48). When we're in partnership with Jesus, "astonishing" things begin to happen.

I recall a flight from Frankfurt, Germany. Carolyn and I were on the first leg of the flight to Boston, followed by a flight to Boise and home.

It had been an exhausting week of ministry for both of us and we were weary. I dropped off to sleep as soon as the plane took off, but was awakened in a few moments by a disturbance in the aisle.

The attendant and a passenger seated on Carolyn's left were arguing about the man's seat assignment. Somehow he had been separated from his fiancée who was several rows behind us.

The man grew increasingly angry and argumentative until another passenger, seated by the man's fiancée, offered to trade places. The swap was made and

Carolyn's new seat-mate settled into his place, drew out a legal pad and began to work on some project.

As it happened, there was a little French boy seated on his left who wanted to talk. The man, who seemed to be the soul of patience, gave up his project after a few minutes and began to chat amiably with the garrulous child. Carolyn was soon drawn into the conversation.

I heard the man say he was from Los Gatos, California, a town close to Los Altos, California, where Carolyn and I had lived for eighteen years. He was on his way to San Francisco. I heard Carolyn remark on the fact that we had many friends in the Bay Area and then I went back to sleep.

When I awakened an hour later I found Carolyn sharing her faith with her new friend, scribbling on his pad of paper, drawing diagrams, animating her story. He was listening intently and asking questions. I sat there quietly and prayed for her and the man.

At one point he said, "You believe as my wife does."

"Oh?" Carolyn replied. "And how did she become a believer?"

"Through Bible Study Fellowship," he responded.

"How did she get into Bible Study Fellowship?" Carolyn asked.

"A friend of hers, Nel King, invited her to attend."

"That's amazing!" Carolyn exclaimed. "Nel King is one of my best friends!"

And then the coin dropped: A few months before we moved to Boise, Nel King had asked Carolyn to pray for a friend who had just become a Christian through Bible Study Fellowship and for her husband who was not yet a believer—the man now seated on Carolyn's left—irresistibly drawn into her net.

Here was Gennesaret all over again.

> The lifelong night we've toiled in vain,
> But at Thy gracious word,
> I will let down the net again:—
> Do Thou Thy will, O Lord.

—John Keble

CHAPTER 23 | A COMFORT

A sweet attractive kind of grace . . .
Continuall comfort in a face.

—MATTHEW ROYDON (1586)

READ Colossians 4:7–11

PAUL WRITES OF CERTAIN FRIENDS WHOM, HE SAYS, "HAVE PROVED a comfort to me." The word *comfort* is an unusual word, a medical term Paul may have picked up from his good friend Dr. Luke. This is the only place it occurs in the New Testament.

In Paul's day the verb meant "to alleviate pain." We get the archaic term "paregoric" from it, a word my mother used to apply to some mysterious and wondrous potion in our medicine chest that was supposed to rid the body of any and every pain.

Paul couldn't have used a better word. What could be more encouraging than to know that there are people like that: men and women who alleviate and mitigate our pain.

Pain is one of the necessities of life. No one evades it. Physical discomfort is hard to bear, but it seems to me that the greatest pain comes from the heart: the pain of weakness and shame; the pain of misunderstanding, criticism and accusation; the pain of deferred hope, disillusionment, and abandoned dreams; the pain of lonely isolation.

Unfortunately there are those sincere but much too certain people who only add to our pain. Like Job's comforters, they talk too much and have a reason for everything that comes our way. They leave us more uncomfortable than before.

On the other hand, there are those good and honest souls who, like Paul's friends, alleviate our pain. Often they're simple, humble people, not in the least important or distinguished, yet somehow in the wear and tear of life they always find a way to reduce our discomfort. It's not that they say very much; it's just that they're there and care and listen well and pray. Most times that's all a body needs.

At other times it's the way they bear their own pain. Their sorrow, endured in simple faith, helps us to bear ours. Their affliction, endured courageously, helps us to be a little braver.

Often they're not even aware of the comfort they bring to us. They're unconscious of any effect because they aren't trying to have an effect. They're just being what they are—a comfort.

You say, "I'd like to be that kind of person." Not to worry. If you're spending time in devotion to God and growing toward likeness to him, you will be a comfort to others whether you know it or not. It's not something you try to do. It's something that happens when you're hiding yourself in him.

It may be that someday someone will write you a letter like Paul did and say, "You were a comfort to me." Maybe not. Some folks never think to tell you what you've done for them or thank you for your consolation. But God knows, and that's all that matters.

CHAPTER 24 | THE WORK OF OUR HANDS

Life is a vapor, but that is long enough to do
the right thing.

—RICHARD SWENSEN

READ Psalm 90:1–17

THE BREVITY AND FLIMSINESS OF LIFE HAVE INSPIRED NUMEROUS metaphors in literature. Human existence is compared to a dream, a flying shuttle, a mist, a puff of smoke, a shadow, a gesture in the air, a sentence written in the sand, a spray of flowers that wither and die in the wind.

In one famous passage, the Venerable Bede, a seventh-century English monk, portrays our life span "as though a sparrow flew swiftly through the hall, coming in by one door and out by the other." We pass through and on. "The life of man is hasty," says Thomas Hobbes.

Like Moses I'm getting a little long in the tooth and thinking more about the brevity of life these days and how little time I have to put my mark on the world. "Will there be some enduring evidence that I've been here?" I ask myself. "Will I leave anything behind that prolongs my usefulness?" Or will I be "time's eunuch," as Gerard Manley Hopkins lamented, and "breed not one work that wakes"?

I think of an ancient pioneer cemetery in the mountains near our home, with gravestones standing like small, slope-shouldered sentinels guarding the human remains. The stones enshrine what's left on earth of men and women who were born, who grew up, married, reared children, made something of themselves, got old and died. Most of the stones have no inscriptions to denote that person's worth—names and dates and little more. All are forgotten. I ask myself, "Is this all that will remain of me—a little mound of Christian dust?"

No one wants to be that useless. So I pray with Moses, "Teach us to number our days aright, that we may gain a heart of wisdom" (90:12).

Our days are numbered—seventy years or so—and then we "fly away," as Moses put it. "Time flies," we say. "No, *you* fly," Time says. Like a bird on the wing we pass swiftly in and out of sight and then we're gone from this earth forever! Now that's something to think about!

Odd isn't it that we try so hard *not* to think about death, when God insists that we do so. But we need to face our dying because that's how we "gain a heart of wisdom."

Medieval monks, I'm told, used to keep human skulls in their cells bearing the Latin inscription *Summus Moribundus* ("We are destined to die") to keep themselves focused on reality. A death sentence, as Samuel Johnson noted, focuses the mind mightily.

Once we grasp the fact that "we're not long for this world," we may begin to wise up. Hopefully, we'll add up the days of our lives, reckon their number to be few and determine by God's grace to make them count while we can. In the words of a plaque that used to hang over my mother's desk:

> Only one life will soon be past;
> Only what's done for Christ will last.
>
> And when I am dying how glad I will be,
> That the lamp of my life has been burned out for Thee.

Moses does affirm that death, though it's something to be reckoned with, is nothing to be feared. He prays with bold assurance: "Satisfy us in the morning [when we "wake up"] with your unfailing love, that we may sing for joy and be glad all our days" (Psalm 90:14). (Also note 90:5: "You sweep men away in the *sleep* of death.")

There is going to be a "great gettin' up morning" when the sun of righteousness will rise with healing in his wings and we will rise with him. Having that hope makes us glad "all our days" here on earth. The world and its passions will pass away, but we who are in Christ will not! We will "live forever" (1 John 2:17).

Death, thus, is nothing to fear; it's easy going. We can forget about our dying and every other deadly thing in the world, rejoice in our eternal life and give ourselves to things that, like us, will endure forever.

One thing that lasts is growth in grace. Peter urges us to "make every effort to add to (our) faith goodness; and to goodness, knowledge; and to knowledge, self-control; and to self-control, perseverance; and to perseverance, godliness; and to godliness, brotherly kindness; and to brotherly kindness, love. For," he concludes, "if [we] possess these qualities in increasing measure, they will keep [us] from being ineffective and unproductive . . ." (2 Peter 1:5–8).

Augustine said, "Do you wish to be great? Then begin by *being*." Enduring greatness stems from what we are. Though we may seem to be doing nothing worthwhile we can be doing everything worthwhile if our lives are being styled by his grace. Set aside through sickness or seclusion we can still be productive. Bed-ridden or house-bound our holiness can still bear fruit.

This can only happen, of course, as we abide in Jesus and he abides in us and we have within us his "indwelling, outgoing fountain store." Only then can we have the fruit that "remains" (John 15:16).

The other lasting thing we can do is to touch as many as possible with God's love—through the words we utter, the prayers we breathe, the letters we write, the counsel we give, the gifts we bestow, the kindness and compassion we show. These are acts of righteousness and compassion, the psalmist says, and they will "endure *forever*" (Psalm 112:2, 9).

> The upright man shines as a light in the darkness—
> > the man who is gracious, compassionate and righteous . . . .
> The righteous man will be remembered *forever* (Psalm 112:4–6).

Actually, it seems to me, the only reason we're left here on earth after salvation and not taken straight to heaven is because God yet has work for us to do. Paul says of himself,

> If I am to go on living in the body, this will mean fruitful labor for me. Yet what shall I choose? I do not know! I am torn between the two: I desire to depart and be with Christ, which is better by far (for me); but it is more necessary for you that I remain in the body. Convinced of this, I know that I will remain, and I will continue with all of you for your progress and joy in the faith . . . (Philippians 1:22–25).

Paul lingered because God had something for him to do: to work with the believers in Philippi for their "progress and joy in the faith." There were Christians in Philippi whose hearts had not yet thoroughly been overtaken by God. Paul was needed. There was work to be done. He would "remain and continue" until his job was finished.

"We are immortal," Augustine said, "until our work is done." The time of our death is not determined by anyone or anything here on earth—not our physicians, not the actuarial tables. That decision is made in the councils of heaven. When we have done all God has in mind for us to do, then and only then will he take us home. As Paul put it, in his sermon at Antioch, "When David had served God's purpose in his own generation, he fell asleep" (Acts 13:36)—and not one second before.

In the meantime, until God takes us home, there's plenty to do. "As long as it is day, we must do the work of him who sent me," Jesus said. "Night is coming, when no one can work" (John 9:4). Night is coming when we will once for all close our eyes on this world, or our Lord will bring this world to a close. Each day brings one of those two conclusions a little closer.

As long as we have the light of day, we must work—not to conquer, acquire, accumulate, and retire, but to make visible the invisible Christ and to touch men and women, boys and girls with his love. If we have done these things, we will have done all we can do and we can rest easy. No matter what else we've done or have not done, our "labor in the Lord" will not be "in vain" (1 Corinthians 15:58).

So Moses prays, "May the favor [beauty] of the Lord our God rest upon us; establish [make permanent] the work of our hands for us—yes, establish [make permanent] the work of our hands" (Psalm 90:17).

This is my prayer as well: May God breathe beauty into your life; may he give permanence to the work of your hands; may your righteousness endure *forever*.

He will do it! "God is able to make all grace abound to you, so that in all things at all times, having all that you need, you will abound in *every* good work" (2 Corinthians 9:8).

CHAPTER 25 | THEY CALL THE HILL MORIAH

His son the father offered up,
Son of his age, his only son,
Object of all his joy and hope,
And less beloved than God alone.

—JOHN WESLEY

READ Genesis 22:1–19

WE KEEP THINKING THAT THINGS WILL GET BETTER AS WE GET ALONG in years, but that's a fool's dream. Sometimes the hardest tests are farther along.

Yet, in another of God's odd reversals, it may be that the worse life gets, the better it can become. Take Abraham, as an example, and his latter days.

After decades of difficulty, Abraham was at last settling into the good life. Ishmael, who had caused so much trouble in the family, had gone off to start a new life. Abraham and Sarah had settled into godly ease and affluence and were enjoying their golden years with Isaac, their love and laughter.

One night the old man crawled into the sack and went off to sleep, oblivious to everything but thankfulness and joy—only to be awakened in the middle of the night by God's call:

"Abraham!"

"Here I am."

"Take your son, your only son, Isaac, whom you love, and go to the region of Moriah. Sacrifice him there as a burnt offering on one of the mountains I will tell you about."

This was "*the* God" as the text makes poignantly clear—the same God who had been so good to Abraham—who now delivers this awful line: "Take your *son* . . . your *only* son . . . the son you *love*, and put him to death."

Isaac was the promised one through whom God pledged to make Abraham great, the son who insured his father's place in the world, Abraham's last hope. He had already lost one son, Ishmael. Would God take another? It made no sense at all.

Abraham knew that the gods of the Chaldeans and Canaanites demanded human sacrifice. How could he know at this juncture that his God would not demand his first-born? *Well*, Abraham must have thought, *it's come to this.*

Yet when morning came, despite his heartache and confusion, Abraham got up and got going, unlike me, inclined as I am to quibble with God when he asks me to do something disagreeable or dangerous. "Certainly not this?" I ask as I look for a loophole, some alternative to faith.

Not Abraham. He went out and found his wedge and maul and began to split wood for the fire, though every stroke must have driven the pain deeper into his heart. Then he saddled his donkey, loaded up the wood and other supplies, and went off with Isaac and two of his servants to a place only God knew—a mountain later called Moriah.

On the third day of his journey Abraham saw the mountain. He said to his servants, "Stay here with the donkey while I and the boy go over there. We will worship and then we will come back to you" (Genesis 22:5).

This was not an empty assurance. Abraham had been thinking along the way. He had recently come to know Yahweh as the "Eternal God" and to remember that revelation had planted a tamarisk tree—a hardy bush that appears to live forever (Genesis 21:33). He concluded that since he and Isaac were joined to God, they too would live forever, and he reckoned that God could and would raise his son from the dead (Hebrews 11:19).

So, taking his leave of the servants, the two—father and son—trudged together, up the mountain (see Genesis 22:7–8).

"Father?"

"Yes, my son?"

"The fire and wood are here, but where is the lamb?"

"God will provide."

There's such marvelous simplicity in that statement and at the same time such depth. This is the answer to every one of life's dilemmas: "God will provide." Sometimes the simplest things are the profoundest things of all.

The two men finally reached the summit where Abraham gathered a few rocks and built an altar stone by stone. He laid the fire, bound Isaac and placed his son—unresisting—on the pyre. Then he lifted his knife . . .

"Abraham! Abraham!"

"Here I am."

"Do not lay a hand on the boy. Do not do anything to him. Now I know that you fear God, because you have not withheld from me your son, your only son."

Then Abraham saw the ram of God, caught by its horns in a bush, and offered it instead of Isaac. And Abraham called the place Moriah ("The LORD Will Provide"), a memory that became a motto forever. Even to this day it is said: "On the Mountain of the LORD it will be provided" (see Genesis 22:11–12).

What did this ordeal mean to Abraham and God? Only that there was *nothing* between them—no greater love.

Perhaps you're being led up Moriah, being asked to kill some dream, some deep desire. You stare in stark unbelief at the thing God is asking you to do. "Is this what he's asking of me? Can this be his will?" you cry out. "Why? Why should this happen to me?"

It's not so difficult to endure these killings when we see the reason, but when God's will defies logic, when it seems contrary to all that's good for us and others, that's when our love is put to the test.

There's love and logic in all that God does. He knows us well. He sees the things that grip our hearts and tear us away from his love. Like Tolkien's Gollum we have our "Precious"—passions that twine themselves around our hearts and strangle them. He wants to tear us from all our preoccupation with ourselves and everything that is ours—our reasonings, our plans, our aspirations; our dreams, our schemes, our visions—all we call "our own." He wants to take us to the place where there is no other love between us and make us "more his" than ever before. Only then can he satisfy us.

Fenelon writes, "[God] wants the 'Isaac' of your heart—the only son, the beloved. He wants you to yield up to Him all that you hold most dear. Until you do this you will have no rest. 'Who is He that has resisted the Almighty and been at peace?' Do you want God to bless you? Give up everything to Him and He will be with you. What comfort, what freedom, what strength, what growth when self-love no longer stands between you and God."

Like Abraham we cannot pick the method, the time, or the place of our Moriah. Only God knows; he must choose and we must let him. It's easier to bear our losses if we accept them without struggling to escape them. We only make life more difficult for ourselves when we resist God—even in the slightest way.

Dying is a terribly unique and personal thing. No one can do it for us; it's something that we must do. "Take *your* son," God said to Abraham. But when we give our Isaac—our only hope—to God, he will give us more than we ever hoped for.

It's significant to me that when Abraham gave his son back to God, God promised again that he would bless all nations through Abraham (Genesis 22:16–19). Now, God said, you will be fruitful beyond your wildest dreams.

God's gifts are of no value to us or to anyone else until we lose them. When we come to the place that God means more to us than anything else, when we love him with all our strength and soul and mind and spirit and heart, when we give up the very gift God has given us, then in resurrection power that gift will bring blessing to everyone it touches.

Perhaps God has richly gifted you for ministry, but has placed you on the shelf. Remember Abraham and offer up those gifts to God. Face the possibility of never using them again. Be content with the Giver alone. He will provide. He will use you in a new and better way—perhaps in a quieter, hidden way—to enrich many.

Perhaps God has called you to another place. You must give up family, friends, home and ministry—every comfort zone—and make another place for yourself. This is Moriah. "On the Mountain of the LORD it will be provided." Beyond the loneliness and soul-ache lies a new and better life. God will use you to bring righteousness and peace in that place.

This is the story of all whose lives have ever counted for God. They have been willing to put to death the very thing they believed was God's gift to them and have contented themselves with God himself. In so doing, he has made them a source of unique and profound blessing to all they know.

This is the paradox of the cross: "He who finds his life will lose it, and he who loses his life for my sake will find it" (Matthew 10:39). "The end of a matter is better than its beginning," the Wise Man says (Ecclesiastes 7:8).

———

About a thousand years after Abraham offered Isaac on Moriah, David bought the entire mountain from Arauvnah, the Canaanite (1 Chronicles 21:15). In David's day Moriah was little more than a scrub-covered, windswept hill. Today Jerusalem straddles the mountain.

Moriah is not a single peak, but an elongated ridge that begins at the junction of the Kidron and Hinnom Valleys in the south and rises to its peak just north-west of the present Damascus Gate. Jesus was crucified there—on the summit of Mount Moriah.

No one reading about old Abraham leading his dear son up the mountain can fail to miss the parallel with God, his own heart breaking, leading his "one and only Son" up Calvary's mountain to the place of the Skull (John 19:17).

Nothing is said about Isaac's inner struggle, but it must have been intense—a picture for us of Jesus' awful turmoil in the Garden of Gethsemane when he faced this very dilemma. God was requiring something which he surely could not be asking. Jesus agonized over that will, sweating, as it were, great drops of blood.

Jesus, like Isaac, was led by his Father to the top of Mount Moriah, bearing the wood of the sacrifice, stumbling under its weight. Jesus, like Isaac, did not open his mouth, but voluntarily was bound to the wood. "He was led like a lamb to the slaughter, and as a sheep before her shearers is silent, so he did not open his mouth" (Isaiah 53:7). Jesus, unlike Isaac, paid the price instead of Isaac and the rest of us. "For the Son of Man did not come to be served, but to serve, and to give his life as a ransom for [instead of] many" (Mark 10:45).

This is the answer to Isaac's question: "Where is the lamb?"—a question asked repeatedly for 2,000 years until Jesus came. He is "the Lamb of God that takes away the sins of the world."

This is the answer to Micah's question, "With what shall I come before the Lord and bow down before the exalted God? . . . Shall I offer my firstborn for my transgression, the fruit of my body for the sin of my soul?" (Micah 6:6–7).

No, God does not require our first born, because he offered up his Son, his *only* Son, the Son that he *loved* (John 3:16).

Remember the Angel's word? "Now I know that you fear God, because you have not *withheld* from me your son, your only son" (Genesis 22:12). Paul writes, using the same Greek word from the Septuagint (the earliest Greek version of the Old Testament) and clearly thinking of this verse: "He who *did not spare* his own

Son, but gave him up for us all—how will he not also, along with him, graciously give us all things?" (Romans 8:32).

God spared Abraham's son; he did not spare his own. Because that is true, will he not give us all things?

CHAPTER 26 | THE BUSINESS OF PRAYER

Seeing me empty, you forsake
The Listener's role, and through
My dead lips breathe and into utterance
    wake
The thoughts I never knew.

—C. S. LEWIS

READ Genesis 18:16–33

I WAS RAISED IN A RELIGIOUS TRADITION THAT PRAYED. WE PRAYED before meals, before meetings, before bedtime, before football games, and before rodeos (to "that Big Cowboy in the sky").

I had no doubt that prayer did something. I just wasn't sure what it was. And, I must confess, even after all these years, I'm still a bit confused. I don't fully understand how prayer works.

Certainly, when push comes to shove, we pray whether we understand prayer or not. It springs from us impulsively and instinctively in the face of necessity. There are no atheists in foxholes, they say, nor in any other holes we dig for ourselves. When we're frightened out of our wits, when we're pushed beyond our limits, when we're pulled out of our comfort zones, we reflexively and involuntarily resort to prayer.

Some years ago I came across a bit of whimsy that enshrines that truth.

> "The proper way for a man to pray,"
>   Said Deacon Lemuel Keyes,
> "And the only proper attitude
>   Is down upon his knees."
>
> "No, I should say the way to pray,"
>   Said Reverend Doctor Wise,
> "Is standing straight with outstretched arms
>   And rapt and upturned eyes."
>
> "Oh, no, no, no," said Elder Slow,
>   "Such posture is too proud.
> A man should pray with eyes fast-closed
>   And head contritely bowed."

"It seems to me his hands should be
　Austerely clasped in front
With both thumbs pointing toward the ground,"
　Said Reverend Doctor Blunt.

"Last year I fell in Hidgekin's well
　Headfirst," said Cyrus Brown,
"With both my heels a-stickin' up
　And my head a-pointin' down.

"And I made a prayer right then and there,
　The best prayer I ever said,
The prayingest prayer I ever prayed,
　A-standin' on my head."

Yes, indeed. In *extremes*, we pray. "The natural thing is to go straight to the Father's knee," as George MacDonald said.

Yet the questions remain, or at least they do for me. How does prayer work? God is perfect wisdom. Does he need me to tell him what to do? He is complete goodness. Does he need me to prod him into doing the right thing? He is infinite wisdom. Does he need my counsel? Is it possible I can ask in such a way that God must change some vast eternal plan? Can I bend his ear and bend his will to mine?

In the midst of all my uncertainty, however, one sure thing remains: prayer changes *me*. It's one of the ways by which God turns me from the things that break my heart to the things that break his.

Take, for example, the story of Abraham and his intercession for the city of Sodom. It has particular value in understanding how prayer works, I believe, at least in terms of the way it works on me.

The story begins with God's verdict on Sodom: "How great is the outcry against Sodom and Gomorrah and how very grave their sin!" (Genesis 18:20 NRSV). The Hebrew idiom underlying this statement can literally be rendered, "the sinners were in the LORD's face," suggesting a flagrant "in your face" attitude, a city raising its puny little fists in defiance of God.

For us Sodom was a sorry little city with no social value and worthy of nothing but immediate and catastrophic judgment; but for Abraham, Sodom was flesh and blood people whom he knew and loved. Abraham had walked the streets of Sodom. He had talked with its citizens. He knew them by name. His nephew and family lived in the city. He had, on one occasion, delivered Sodom from a gang of thugs. It wasn't easy for him to give up Sodom, wicked though it was. Abraham grieved for its people.

God knew Abraham's aching heart and knew he must talk with his friend before he acted in judgment, so he and two of his angels clothed themselves with flesh and came to visit Abraham under the Oaks of Mamre.

They came bearing a gift, as visitors sometimes do, the promise that Sarah would give birth to a long-awaited son. That business done, the Lord and his angels got up to leave and Abraham, with the politeness of a good Semitic host, got up to go with them.

Abraham, the Lord, and the two angels trudged along for some distance in silence while the Lord communed with himself:

> Shall I hide from Abraham what I am about to do? Abraham will surely become a great and powerful nation, and all nations on earth will be blessed through him. For I have chosen him, so that he will direct his children and his household after him to keep the way of the Lord by doing what is right and just, so that the Lord will bring about for Abraham what he has promised him (Genesis 18:17–19).

Here in this soliloquy we see God's heart, his desire to let his dear friend Abraham in on his deepest secrets. "Is not this the time to take Abraham into my deepest counsel?" he says to himself.

Was this disclosure necessary because Abraham was a superior being, more in touch with God than all the rest of us? No, indeed. God longs to reveal his heart to everyone he loves: "Surely the Sovereign Lord does nothing without revealing his plan to his servants," one of the servants said (Amos 3:7). He does so because that's what one does for a friend.

Friends open their hearts to one another; they hold nothing back. "I have called you friends," Jesus said to his disciples, "for *everything* that I learned from my Father I have made known to you" (John 15:15).

So, when the angels turned away and went toward Sodom, "the Lord remained standing before Abraham." Unfortunately, most versions render the text, "Abraham remained standing before the Lord" (Genesis 18:22), but that's a crashing mistake. The traditional Hebrew text states just the opposite: "the Lord remained standing before Abraham."

Apparently, some scribe had trouble with the notion of God standing before Abraham like someone waiting for a handout and reinterpreted the text mightily to accommodate his own theology. Emendations like this rarely occurred in those days, and when they did, the scribes hardly ever altered the actual text, but placed their changes in the margin—something to be read, they said, in place of what was written. Unfortunately, in this case the alteration found its way into the text itself and then into our modern translations.

The original version, however, tells us that God was actually standing before Abraham, patiently waiting for him to speak. As written, the text underscores God's passion to communicate with all of us. He, as in Abraham's day, stands continually before us, drawing us out, listening to our hearts and waiting to reveal his own.

"Prayer is [God's] idea," Lloyd Ogilvie says. "[Our] desire to pray is the result of his greater desire to talk with us. *He* has something to say when we feel the urge to pray."

What follows, then, is the well-known account of that conversation between Abraham and God, with Abraham pleading Sodom's case, begging the Lord to spare Sodom for the sake of a few righteous souls, and God agreeing for that number to spare it.

Abraham is faulted at times for his unwillingness to persist in his intercession, to wring Sodom's salvation from God for the sake of his nephew Lot (who, it appears, was the only good man in town). But, believe me, Abraham was never lacking in gumption and certainly not on this occasion. No, Abraham stopped praying because for the first time he saw the situation from God's point of view. At every step God's justice loomed larger; at every step more of God's justice entered into the man. In the end he was thinking more like God than ever before.

Here's the point: Abraham's prayer for Sodom didn't change anything—except Abraham. God had determined to judge that audacious sin-city because there was nothing in it worth saving. By prayer Abraham entered into God's wisdom, understood his thinking, and by it became a little more like God.

Prayer, then, whatever else it may be, is not calling God's attention to things he's not aware of, nor is it urging him to do his duty. No, it's a conversation in which we speak our mind and God speaks his. We talk and we listen until we get into his mind and he gets into ours.

All of which means that when we get down to praying, we don't have to worry about what to say or how to say it. We can say whatever is in us. Though our prayers may spring from anxious fear or angry, ungodly thoughts of personal revenge, God will take those prayers into his heart and turn them into something else, and in the process he will turn us into something else.

I think that's what Paul meant when he wrote: "Do not be anxious about anything, but in everything, by prayer and petition, with thanksgiving, present your requests to God. And the peace of God, which transcends all understanding, will guard your hearts and your minds in Christ Jesus" (Philippians 4:6–7).

There's no promise here that anything or anyone is changed by our prayers except our state of mind. God's tranquility takes the place of our anxiety; his peace transcends our panic. Prayer, thus, wrung out of us by our deepest needs, has been turned into something yet more profound. In our praying *we* have been transformed.

This is God at work. This is the business of prayer.

CHAPTER 27 | QUAGMIRE

Oh, the sots and thralls of lust
Do in spare hours more thrive than I that
    spend,
Sir, life upon Thy cause.

—GERARD MANLEY HOPKINS

READ 1 Thessalonians 4:1–8

"LUST IS A QUAGMIRE," A FRIEND OF MINE SAID RECENTLY. *QUAGMIRE* is exactly the right word. Lust bogs us down and keeps us from making any progress toward God.

I always think in this connection of one of my favorite trout streams here in Idaho. It's a beautiful little spring creek, braided with bright green moss and water weed, flowing down a narrow valley through willows and wild Russian olives. The trout in that stream are big and strong.

However, the river has a dark side. The bottom is soft silt and decaying vegetable matter—soft, sticky stuff that mires you down and holds you fast. Several times I've become so stuck in the mud that I couldn't move and had to call to one of my fishing-friends to pull me out. At times I've had to do the same for them. I don't fish that creek much by myself. It's not at all safe.

The danger beneath the beauty and enjoyment of that little stream has become for me a parable of the things that impede our progress and prevent our enjoyment of God. Sexual impurity is one of those things that can leave us "stuck."

Here in this text Paul puts the matter squarely before us, "It is God's will that you should be sanctified: that you should avoid sexual immorality" (1 Thessalonians 4:3). The two ideas—sanctification and sexual immorality—are juxtaposed as polar opposites. We can make no progress toward godliness as long as we're mired in immorality. The one necessarily precludes the other.

The word Paul uses in this text, translated "sexual immorality" is the Greek word *porneia* from which we get our word *fornication*. Fornication is a perfectly good word, but unfortunately it's a used-up word, associated as it is with thoughts of quaint and hoary prudery. We need to recapture its meaning.

Our English word "fornication" comes from a Latin term *fornix* that originally referred to a cellar, and then by extension to buying sex, since brothels in Rome were located in cellars and other low-down places. The Greek word that lies behind the English word had the same connotation. It meant "to buy" or "to sell" and then came to be used of prostitution. A harlot was called a *pornei*—one who was bought and sold.

George Bernard Shaw tells about an encounter with a young woman whom he approached on a drunken whim. "Would you sleep with me for a thousand pounds?" he whispered.

"I would," she replied.

"Would you sleep with me for five pounds?" Shaw teased.

"Sir," she replied angrily, "what do you think I am?"

"Well," Shaw chuckled, "we've already established that. Now we're just haggling over the price."

That's exactly the point: fornication is a sell-out, and though few will admit it, we all have our price. If we don't think so, we're fools and headed for a terrible fall. Every one of us is only thirty minutes or less away from ruin.

The best illustration of the word *fornication* is supplied in a context that has nothing to do with sexual matters. The writer to the Hebrews encourages us to pursue God and the holiness that flows from that pursuit (12:15–16, emphasis added):

> See to it that no one misses the grace of God and that no bitter root [of rebellion against God] grows up to cause trouble and defile many. See that no one is sexually immoral, or is godless like Esau, who for a single meal *sold his inheritance rights* as the oldest son.

Esau came in from a hard day of hunting, exhausted and craving a meal. His appetite was so strong that he traded away his birthright—his part in God's plan to bring salvation to the world—for the immediate gratification of a physical craving. He prostituted his priceless inheritance for a quick meal (Genesis 25:29–34).

Sexual immorality is exactly that. We give away something eternally valuable and completely satisfying for immediate physical gratification. God wants to fill and flood our bodies and use them as his instruments to touch the world in profound and lasting ways, but immorality frustrates that purpose. We "bid farewell to our greatness," Shakespeare said.

Paul continues his argument: "Each one of us should learn to control his own body in a way that is holy and honorable, not in passionate lust like the heathen, who do not know God" (1 Thessalonians 4:4–5).

Here's a straightforward plea for self-control, based on the knowledge of God. Ordinary men are driven by lust because they do not know God. God's men and women know God and therefore have another passion: to present their bodies to him for his purposes.

Real Christians are different from others, not merely in degree but in kind. They have God and others do not. Because they have God they have a bent toward righteousness—a proclivity toward purity and holiness—and when they fail in that pursuit, they feel it and know it.

But here's the rub: though they know what it is to be holy, they cannot be holy by direct effort. That's a job for God. If we are to master our lustful passions, it will be done through his efforts alone. There is no other way.

C. S. Lewis explains the process this way:

> Put right out of your head the idea that . . . Christians are to read what Christ said and try to carry it out—as a man may read what Plato or Marx said and try to carry it out. They mean something much more than that. They mean that a real Person, Christ, here and now, in that very room where you are saying your prayers, is doing things to you. It is not a question of a good man who died two thousand years ago. It is a living Man, still as much a man as you, and still as much God as He was when He created the world, really coming and interfering with your very self; killing the old natural self in you and replacing it with the kind of self He has. At first, only for moments. Then for longer periods. Finally, if all goes well, turning you permanently into a different sort of thing; into a new little Christ, a being which, in its own small way, has the same kind of life as God; which shares in His power, joy, knowledge and eternity.

Turning us into "a different sort of thing" takes time—actually a lifetime. What God wants is for us to give him our bodies so he can begin the process right now. It's not what we make of ourselves that matters, but what God is making of us. We're a work in progress and will remain so until we go to God or until he comes for us. Then and only then will his work be done.

We see life piece-meal—like a bug working its way along a clothesline. God sees what we will be when we get to the end of the line. Until that day comes we must keep inching along, making a little progress every day, upheld by his faithfulness, assured by his forgiveness and encouraged by his promise that we will someday be what he has called us to be.

"The one who calls you is faithful," Paul assures us, "and *he* will do it" (1 Thessalonians 5:24).

CHAPTER 28 | YOU AIN'T SEEN NOTHIN' YET!

His grace is sufficient; we walk not alone;
As the day, so the strength that he gives to
his own.

—Annie Johnson Flint

READ Jeremiah 12:1–6

I READ SOMEWHERE THAT CARL LEWIS WAS ONCE CHALLENGED TO a foot race with a horse. It's been done before: Jim Thorpe, "The World's Greatest Athlete," actually out-sprinted a thoroughbred—at least for a few yards.

I suppose Lewis turned the offer down. I've heard nothing of the outcome. It was enough for him, I imagine, to have run with men. But all of this got me to thinking about something God once said to Jeremiah: "If you have raced with men on foot and they have worn you out, how can you compete with horses? If you stumble in safe country, how will you manage in the thickets by the Jordan?" (Jeremiah 12:5).

The background to this text is significant. Judah's good king Josiah, in a rare display of stupidity, tried to take on Pharaoh Necho of Egypt and his entire army, and he got himself killed in the process. That put Judah back into the hands of the old guard—the idolatrous prophets and priests whom Jeremiah had attacked for years. They quietly put out a contract on the prophet's life.

At first Jeremiah knew nothing of the conspiracy, since he was preaching in the little villages of Judah. But he soon learned of it and fled to Anathoth, his hometown, where he hoped to find sanctuary. But it wasn't to be. Even there Jeremiah wasn't safe. His neighbors conspired to kill him.

The prophet began to cry the blues: "You are always righteous, O LORD, when I bring a case before you. . . . [But] why does the way of the wicked prosper?" (Jeremiah 12:1). I know the tune. I've sung it myself many times.

The Lord's answer was an unexpected, gentle rebuke (my paraphrase): "If you can't run with men, Jeremiah, how can you run with horses? If you can't thrive in the relative safety of the city, what will you do in the wilderness"—where bears, lions, and other predators prowled (see Jeremiah 12:5).

It occurred to me, while reading this exchange, that God and I often work at odds with one another: I want my detractors to lighten up, but God wants me to toughen up. "If you can't deal with what's coming down the road today," he seems to be saying, "how can you handle the heavy traffic tomorrow?"

It seems that God is busy preparing all of us for greater things. He does so by giving us the opportunity to trust him in our present difficulties so that our faith will grow stronger and more muscular for the greater difficulties to come. His presence in our trouble today gives us strength for the double-trouble tomorrow.

It's good to know, however, that while God is preparing us for greater things tomorrow, he won't push us over the edge today. He won't challenge us to race against horses until he's taught us to run with men. He won't send us into the "thickets of the Jordan" to grapple with grizzlies and other beasts until he's shown us his power on less arduous and hazardous occasions.

He brings us along slowly, measuring each trial against our current measure of faith, pushing us, but never pushing us beyond our ability to believe; never giving us more than we can bear, but often giving us more than we *think* we can bear. He proves himself strong in our trouble. That's how we learn that his grace is sufficient for *any* ordeal.

And so I say to myself: "Not to worry. This trial today—whatever it is—is not overwhelming. God's grace is sufficient for me. I can take comfort in his strengthenings."

Furthermore, this trial is given to me today that I may know more of God's grace tomorrow. If greater troubles rise and overshadow me, he will give a *greater* grace. As the day, so his strength shall be.

And though the future brings some heavier cross,
I need not cloud the present with my fears;
I know the grace that is enough today
Will be sufficient still through all the years.

—Annie Johnson Flint

CHAPTER 29 | THE GRAPEVINE

Or cannot leaves, but fruit be signe
Of the true vine?

—George Herbert

READ John 15:1–8

THERE'S AN OLD VINEYARD IN A CANYON THAT I FISH THROUGH
now and then. It was an effort by some Idaho pioneer to grow grapes and make
sweet wine I suppose, but it's long since been abandoned.

I saw it again this winter, and though the gnarled old stocks looked dead to
me, I knew next spring they'd leaf out again and produce grapes. Through all the
years its fruit remains.

That old vineyard always reminds me of Jesus' metaphor: "I am the vine; you
are the branches. If a man remains in me and I in him, he will bear much fruit;
apart from me you can do nothing" (John 15:5).

175

When Jesus uttered these words, he and his disciples were making their way down the east slope of Mount Zion—down the steps that led into the Valley of the Kidron on their way to the Mount of Olives. In that day the entire slope was one vast vineyard, stretching up and down the valley as far as the eye could see. It was the sight of the vines and the branches covered with spring blossoms and a late-working vine keeper or two that probably evoked the metaphor that Jesus uses here.

Jesus saw the vine branches trained along trellises for vast distances, yet, as he knew, one life pervaded and sustained the whole from the oldest root to the farthest twig, leaf, and cluster. He thought of the connection between the vine and branch and the relationship his disciples sustained to him and settled on this symbol: "I am the vine; you are the branches."

We are branches, united to Jesus the vine, integrally joined to him by faith and by God's goodness and grace. His life pervades our being from one end to the other. All that he has is ours for the taking. The result, Jesus insists, is "fruit."

The word *fruit* in the Bible rarely symbolizes souls brought to Christ. Rather it represents personal righteousness—not what we do, but what we *are* (compare Isaiah 5:1–7; Galatians 5:22–23). Fruit, in the natural and biblical sense, is product of the life of the vine, penetrating and perfusing the branches so that something useful is produced. There can be no fruit apart from the vine. As Jesus said, "Without me you can do nothing."

We cannot by moral effort become fruitful. It is the result of daily association with Jesus. It begins with "abiding." Abiding is utter dependence—drawing on

Christ for all that we do. It means sitting at his feet in solitude and surrender, listening for his voice, asking for his counsel, waiting for his impulses in intercession and action, then walking through the world trusting, resting, asking for his help.

Abiding is acknowledging our inadequacy and our inability to change ourselves one iota. It is a moment by moment yielding—not a fatalistic acquiescence or passive resignation, but an active submission of our whole being to Jesus so that his presence and power can be released through our bodies in every circumstance. It is an open receptivity that undergirds all we do.

The result, Jesus says, is fruit—"love, joy, peace, patience, kindness, goodness, faithfulness, gentleness and self-control"—those infused virtues that produce refreshment and healing in others.

Busy lives revolt against abiding. When we allow ourselves to be swept up in every cause and concern, when we surrender to every demand, when we give ourselves to every worthwhile project, when we try to be all things to all people all the time, we have no time to abide—and then we become useless. Like broken and detached branches we wither and die and are good for nothing.

Frenzy destroys the fruit because it disconnects us from the root—that source of goodness and wisdom that marks us and makes us useful. We must be less busy—to take time to be joined to Jesus, that "he may produce in and through us whatever fruit He will for the nourishment of men and the glory of God" (F. B. Meyer).

To allow one's self to be carried away
    by a multitude of conflicting concerns . . .

To surrender to too many demands,
To commit one's self to too many projects,
To want to help everyone in everything
    is to succumb to violence.

Frenzy destroys our inner capacity for peace.

It destroys the fruitfulness of our work.
    because it kills the root of inner wisdom
    which makes work fruitful.

—Thomas Merton

CHAPTER 30 | KILLED WITH A KISS

> Still as of old, men by themselves are
> priced—
> For thirty pieces Judas sold *himself*, not
> Christ.
>
> —Hester H. Cholmondeley

READ Luke 22:47–48

JUDAS HAS COME DOWN TO US AS THE ARCH-FIEND OF HISTORY, the man who betrayed the Lord of Glory. Luke describes him with subtle contempt as "the one called Judas" (22:47 NRSV). Dante, in his *Inferno*, portrays Judas in the lowest reaches of hell, separated from even the cruelest denizens of that dreadful place.

Yet Judas was no monster. He was an ordinary man like you and me with vast potential for good or evil. Where did he go wrong?

To put it simply, Judas loved money. It was his passion, and in the end it consumed him and drew his heart away from God. One master passion swallowed up all the rest.

Two things go wrong with us when we love money. The first is that our hearts are drawn away from *good*. Jesus said, "If your eyes are good, your whole body will be full of light. But if your eyes are bad, your whole body will be full of darkness" (Matthew 6:22–23).

The state of the heart is determined by what we "see." If we set our eyes on money and what it will bring us, our bodies become "full of darkness." We become confused and uncertain, our judgment is clouded and we begin to make unprincipled choices that defy logic and deny our own values. Then we'll do anything to make a buck. The rust and moth that corrupts the treasure has corrupted our souls. The light within us has gone out, and, as Jesus said, "How great is that darkness!" (Matthew 6:23).

Paul says precisely the same thing in another place: "People who *want* to get rich fall into a temptation and a trap and into many foolish and harmful desires that plunge men into ruin and destruction. For the love of money is a root of all kinds of evil" (1 Timothy 6:9–10).

The second problem with loving money is that it draws our hearts away from *God*. "No one can serve two masters. Either he will hate the one and love the other, or he will be devoted to the one and despise the other. You cannot serve God and Money" (Matthew 6:24).

Money deprives us: we lose our vision of God. A man can have only one master passion. If money becomes our fascination, we will lose our fascination with God. Then our hearts will become progressively harder until we turn our backs on the living God. Judas is a prime example.

———————

What do we know of Judas's beginnings? Not much, other than what we're told in the Bible. It appears that he grew up in the little town of Kerioth about twenty-five miles south of Jerusalem. (His surname, Iscariot, probably means "a man of Kerioth.")

Some authorities suggest that Judas's surname, Iscariot, comes from a Latin root, *sicarius,* meaning "assassin." The *Scariotes,* as they were called, were radical zealots bent on driving the Romans from their homeland. But Judas was no radical. He was, if anything, "a good old boy." He didn't create any problems; he went along.

Judas was probably a very bright young man with a head for numbers and a good deal of natural ambition, the sort of person voted "Most Likely to Succeed" by his classmates. He was also the kind of young man most likely to get out of town. The strictures and small minds of his tiny community may have led him to move to the big city as soon as he could. (Kerioth was like that little town in the country-western song whose city limits mark the end of the world, "cause folks leave town and never come back.")

Perhaps Judas came in contact with Jesus in Jerusalem, the big city to which he would most likely go. He listened to our Lord's teaching, hung on every word, watched the crowd grow around Jesus, and realized that this was a man who was going someplace—someone who could make him rich and famous. So Judas became a disciple and at some point was appointed an apostle.

Soon after, Judas was elected treasurer of the group, and shortly after that he began to dip into the till. Then he took more, and greed and avarice consumed him.

That's the way it is with sin: we slide slowly into it. Little by little it hardens our heart. The process of hardening is so deceptive we can't always see it, or sense what's happening to us. We drift away from the knowledge of God in small increments.

Alexander Pope put it well:

> Vice is monster of so frightful mien,
> As to be hated is to be seen.
> Yet seen too often, familiar with her face,
> We first endure, then pity, then embrace.

Judas isn't mentioned much in the Gospels until that event at which a woman poured a flask of perfume "worth a year's wages" over Jesus' head and feet. Judas objected: "Why wasn't this perfume sold and the money given to the poor?" (John 12:5).

It's worth noting that some of the other apostles chimed in at this point, but John notes that Judas didn't protest because he cared for the poor, but "because he was a thief; as keeper of the money bag, he used to help himself to what was put into it" (John 12:4–6). Had the perfume been sold the money would have found its way into Judas's pocket. As it was, he saw a year's wages slip away.

You get the impression from the account that Jesus' rebuke angered Judas. He realized that Jesus' attitude toward money precluded accumulation on his part, and so he decided at that moment to profit from his association in some other way. He went immediately to the chief priests to arrange Jesus' betrayal. Again, it's worth noting that on that occasion Judas "haggled" with the chief priests to get the sweetest deal. Judas was a man who always worked the angles.

Judas had numerous opportunities to respond to Jesus' love. He saw him heal the sick and raise the dead. He saw him lavish his love on outcasts and sinners. He was with him when he hugged that awful leper. He listened to the conversation with the rich young ruler. He heard Jesus speak on numerous occasions about money and the dangers inherent in loving it. (Jesus said more about money than almost anything else.) And there must have been times when Judas looked up to find Jesus gazing at him with incredible love in his eyes.

It has always intrigued me that no one in the Upper Room identified Judas when Jesus made the claim that one of them would betray him. The disciples may have glanced at others around the table, but it appears no one thought of Judas. That suggests that Jesus never betrayed the betrayer—never shunned him; never shamed him; always treated him with love and affection. Yet Judas was impervious to Jesus' love.

John tells us that when Jesus spoke about his betrayal and death in the Upper Room he became "troubled in spirit" (John 13:21). It wasn't the step *he* was about to take that troubled him. It was the step *Judas* was about to take. Our Lord's sensitive soul yearned in pity for the man.

Jesus made one last effort to reach out to the betrayer when he handed him the morsel in the Upper Room—the "sop" that contained pieces of the Pascal Lamb. He was offering himself again to the man. Judas took the morsel and hardened his heart all the more.

Even then Jesus did not betray Judas. He whispered to him, "What you are about to do, do quickly" (John 13:27). Judas rose immediately and "went out," as John reports, "and it was night"—one of the most poignant phrases in the Bible. Satan entered into Judas and the powers of darkness took over. The rest of the story, as they say, is history.

When Jesus was officially condemned to death, Judas, overwhelmed by remorse, tried to undo his deed by returning the money, only to be turned away contemptuously by the priests. (Traitors are despised even by those who profit from their treachery.) Then Judas hanged himself.

I don't know what brought about Judas's remorse. Perhaps it was Jesus' quiet response to his kiss: "Are you betraying the Son of Man with a kiss?" (Luke 22:47). "Son of Man" is a Messianic title and is strongly emphasized in the text. Perhaps the enormity of Judas's treachery came home to him at that moment. He realized he had sold out his Messiah. He could not endure his shame and guilt and so put an end to his life.

It seems clear, however, that Judas did not repent in the biblical sense of the word. There was self-reproach and sorrow, but no humility and contrition and no turning to God for forgiveness. Only regret and self-reproach.

Could Judas have come back? I believe so. There are no limits to God's grace. Judas might have been saved were it not for his suicide. Jerome insisted that Judas saddened our Lord more by hanging himself than by betraying him. How so? Because Judas's suicide put an end to Jesus' efforts to save him.

Calvin concluded that Judas killed himself because he could not believe God could forgive him for what he had done: he "conceived of [him] only as Avenger and Judge" (*Institutes* 1:18.4 and 3:3.4). There may be something to that notion, but I think that the underlying issue was hardness of heart—pride and stubbornness mastered Judas at the end. There are those times when God would, but we *will* not.

Believing as I do in God's grace, I know that Judas could have sought out the risen Savior and taken what forgiveness he needed. Had Judas fallen at Jesus' feet, our Lord would have lifted him up, hugged him, and returned his unfaithful kiss with genuine affection.

George MacDonald, in *The Flight of the Shadow*, tells a story of a little girl, Barbara Whichote, who lived with her uncle and who one day got into his study when he was gone and rummaged through his private and forbidden collection of jewelry. The secret burned inside her for days, until in desperation she came into her uncle's room one night and flung herself down beside his bed. "Please uncle," she sobbed, "will you kill me?"

"Yes, yes," her uncle replied, "I will kill you my darling! Like this! Like this!" Then stretching out his arms he drew her in and covered her face with kisses.

MacDonald concludes with this thought on God's avuncular love: "We have been killed by the kisses of God."

CHAPTER 31 | THE LEGACIES OF TIME

Youth is full of sport;
Age's breathe is short.

—S<small>HAKESPEARE</small>

READ 2 Corinthians 4:16–18

OFF TO THE SOUTH OF IDAHO THERE'S A RANGE OF MOUNTAINS known as The Owyhees, so named because a couple of "Owyhee" (Hawaiian) trappers were killed up there in 1819 by a band of Shoshones. It's a remote region of rugged mountains and deep gorges, rarely visited and located in what I've been told is the least-populated county in the Lower Forty-Eight. It's one of my favorite places, though I don't get up there as much as I'd like to anymore.

Last winter my oldest son, Randy, my grandson, Mark, and I were hiking up a creek in the Owyhees, exploring it for future fishing trips. We came to a side canyon and decided to look into it. It was a rugged little wadi, consisting of a series of small terraces formed by lava dikes, each one more challenging than the last, each one inviting us to make one more ascent. There had to be something up there to see!

We arrived at last at what appeared to be the final wall, this one straight up and too high to scale—at least that was my conviction. Without hesitation, however, Randy and Mark began to scramble up the face, using whatever hand and footholds they could find until they reached the top. It occurred to me as I watched them climb that once you got to the top it was a long way to the bottom.

I watched these two fit, young athletes climb for awhile, wondering whether there was anything up there worth seeing. That's when it came to me: there wasn't! There was absolutely no reason why I needed to make that climb.

While the young men continued their explorations, I found a warm place in the sun to sit down and ponder this sudden conviction. As I sat there (like Abraham contemplating his body as good as dead) it occurred to me that it's actually a good thing to be over the hill. The slope is down now, much easier on the heart and legs.

In the first place, I don't have to be macho anymore. I don't have to make a name for myself. I can sit on the sidelines and watch other people risk life and limb. I can run in the slow lane while others try to out-hustle each other. I can spectate while others jockey for position. I can kick back and let the rest of the world do the derring-do.

That idea immediately associated itself with another thought in my mind: it's also good to be long enough in the tooth to get past the point where I don't have to be good-looking any more. It's easy to look good when you're young, but it gets harder as you get along in years, and then it gets to be impossible.

As I look back, I must say that I devoted too much time to that losing cause. It was a kind of servitude, really, a slavery to myself that inhibited the cultivation of better things. It's good to get past that necessity.

C. S. Lewis once wrote to a friend,

> I do most heartily agree that it is just as well to be past the age when one expects or desires to attract the other sex. It's natural enough in our species as in others that the young birds show off their plumage—in the mating season. But the trouble in the modern world is that there's a tendency to rush all the birds on to that age as soon as possible and then keep them there as late as possible, thus losing all the real value of the other parts of life.

Old age is the season when we can give ourselves to "soul-making," as the Friends say. We can concentrate on getting to know God better and cultivating those character traits that make us more like him. Age breaks down our strength and energy and strips us of our busyness. It's God's way of getting us to slow down so we'll take more time for him. We can think more deeply about life, about ourselves, and about others.

Spiritual growth is a gradual and continual process and one which we must cultivate. That means we must give ourselves time, and time is something we older folks usually have plenty of.

Though older people are sometimes uneasy about change, change is an inevitable part of life. We're being shaped every minute we live. Every thought, every decision, every action, every emotion, every response is shaping us into one kind of person or the other. Either we're moving toward likeness to Christ or away from him into some sort of caricature of the person God intended us to be. We're either becoming more redemptive or more destructive to ourselves and to others. A man can't be static; he has to change—one way or the other.

It's true, we lose some things as we age: physical strength, quickness, agility and other factors "dear to youth, to manhood's prime." But think of the calm God gives us, the peace he leaves us, "the hoarded spoils, the legacies of time."

Old age is the best time to grow in grace and grandeur, in inner strength and beauty of character. "Gray hair," the wise man said, "is a crown of splendor; [a beauty] attained by a righteous life" (Proverbs 16:31).

The other thing about old age is that you have more time to give your wisdom away to others. But some people don't get wiser as they get older; they just get to be old fools. If we are to be useful to others, however, the important thing is to fill ourselves full of God so that we have more of his manner and judgment and less of our own foolishness to give away.

Almost every young man I come across these days is looking for an old grizzly, an older man who'll come alongside and help him come into his own. *Mentor* is usually the word they use. It's a good word, with rich associations.

According to Homer's *Odyssey,* when King Odysseus went off to fight in the Trojan war, he left his son, Telemachus, in the hands of a wise old man named Mentor who was charged with the task of teaching the young man wisdom.

Two thousand years later, the French scholar, François Fenelon, who was the tutor to the grandson of Louis XIV, adapted the story of Telemachus in a novel entitled *The Adventures of Telemachus,* enlarging and popularizing the character of Mentor.

The word *mentor* soon came to have the dictionary meaning of "a wise and responsible tutor," a more experienced person who advises, guides, inspires, challenges, corrects, and serves as a model. The proper name, Mentor, has now become a common noun.

Mentors, however, are anything but common. Timothy had Paul, Mark had Barnabas, Joshua had Moses, Elisha had Elijah, Mary had Elizabeth. But where are those older, wiser men and women who will love beginners and help them transcend their difficulties, who will encourage, guide, teach and model the truth for them and thereby strengthen their grip on God?

Paul said of himself, "Though outwardly we are wasting away, yet inwardly we are being renewed day by day" (2 Corinthians 4:16). If we, like the apostle, keep growing toward God and helping others move in that direction, though our bodies may be declining, our spirits can stay lively and quick. "I can't help getting older," a friend of mine says, "but I don't have to get old."

Years ago I read an introduction to a commentary by Matthew Henry that came to mind as I wrote this final piece: "If I may but be instrumental to make [others] wise and good, wiser and better, more watchful against sin and more careful of their duty both to God and man, . . . more in love with God and His word, I have all I desire, all I aim at."

Who could ask for anything more?

NOTE TO THE READER

THE PUBLISHER INVITES YOU TO SHARE YOUR RESPONSE TO THE message of this book by writing Discovery House Publishers, P.O. Box 3566, Grand Rapids, MI 49501, USA. For information about other Discovery House books, music, DVDs, or videos, contact us at the same address or call 1-800-653-8333. Find us on the Internet at www.dhp.org or send e-mail to books@dhp.org.